I'M O.K.

A Young Mother's Struggle

Sherry L. Pierce

This book is a work of non-fiction. Names and places have been changed to protect the privacy of all individuals. The events and situations are true.

ISBN: 1-4107-0559-5 (e-book)
ISBN: 1-4107-0560-9 (Paperback)

This book is printed on acid free paper.

1stBooks - rev. 1/13/03

"I'M O.K. is a true inspiration to any survivor of a stroke, their loved ones, caregivers, or rehab professionals. As a Speech Therapist who works with these patients on a daily basis, I often forget the personal trials and tribulations that accompany the physical and cognitive deficits resulting from a stroke. Sherry's unbelievable courage and incredible energy are a great example to all people, especially victims of a neurological deficit, that hard work and motivation can definitely pay off in the end. There IS life after a stroke, and sometimes even a better life..."

-Tammy Pierce, M.A., C.C.C.-S.L.P.

"Mental and Physical Toughness, that's what I am talking about! My sister has looked the "Grim Reaper" in the face, drawn a line, and dared him to cross. Sherry possesses great values, which include: Honesty, Integrity, and a most admirable, Personal Courage. Her willingness to go the distance in the face of adversity is immeasurable. She inspires me!"

-Duane A. Pierce, Sherry's Brother

Preface

. . . .

The general purpose of this book in the beginning was only
for me.
I used it as a place to vent my anger and filter my pain.
However, by the time I finished half the manuscript I began
to realize
that my story might give people hope.

My experience will touch many different
people—victims, their families,
caregivers, therapists, friends and doctors;
anyone who has suffered a tragedy similar to mine.

Or
just someone off the street—who I may give the chance to
feel the experience
through my words. Perhaps I can give you an opportunity to
look around, slow down, and appreciate the simpler things
in life.

Most of all, I want to send a message of hope, patience, and
strength to
other victims of strokes. I want you,
your family, and our caregivers
to know that—no matter how bad it gets—
what you do every day in your life makes all the difference.

be trusted, the brain seems to be an astonishingly resilient
organ, and one capable, in certain circumstances, of
remarkable recovery.

I am living proof and I'm OK!

Dedication

This book is
Dedicated to:

....

My beautiful sons

**Codey Dylan
&
Gabriel Jacob**

In loving Memory of

Rachel B. Lee

1952-1977

**"My Aunt"—a mother of two young sons who died
in a fatal accident.**

Chapter 1

Fate – A force that predetermines life's events...

As I sit here on my front porch...I inhale a breath of this sweet country air. Smelling the light aroma of freshly cut grass, I wonder...is this my fate? Who determines a person's fate? Is it GOD? Or can we determine our own fate or destiny?

I'd like to believe that having a stroke at the age of thirty was not predetermined from the beginning of my life.

I believe that tragic events will come to play during each of our lives. What we decide to do with the outcome of these events is, in reality, our fate. GOD is involved at all times, giving the strength to overcome and deal with tragedy.

Of course, it's only human nature to wonder when something bad happens if there was something you could have changed to make events turn out differently. I can't change anything, no matter how stupid my choices were or why I did things? But the bottom line of my story is a miracle, an event that seems impossible to explain by natural laws and so is regarded as an act of GOD.

If I had changed anything in the events that caused my disability, I wouldn't have my miracle: Gabriel.

I will start by saying I'm 31 years old, three times divorced, and the single mother of two beautiful sons. I'm also a stroke survivor. Writing down the words of pain and telling my story on paper has become my best therapy.

My first marriage broke down because I married too young. He was a good man, but it was the wrong time for us both. Luckily, we ended up with a wonderful son and I found two life long friends in my ex- husband and his wife. With my second marriage, I thought he was my last chance for the American dream. because he was established and older. As it turned out, he was just *crazy and older.*

I don't know you could compare my man finding skills to catching snowflakes, every flake is different but they're still flakes.

The real story begins with my third husband. They say the third time is the charm, but not in this case.

When we met, I was five years Shaw's senior and still in the process of divorcing husband number two. I wasn't ready for a new relationship. I should've listened to my stepfather David, who paid attention to the huge red flags waving in front of me. Flags like: *"I don't have a drivers license"* or *"I can't keep a job for more than a month"* or *" I still live with mommy"* or *"Can you drop me off at drug and alcohol class so I can get my license back?"*

Through all the red flags I told myself, I'm having fun with this guy, so why does it matter? I honestly didn't believe we had a future together. Nevertheless, days led into weeks, and weeks led into months. I found a house I really liked and got it in my name, my divorce was final, and life seemed good. I enjoyed my job and made decent money. I worked in the systems programming department for the government processing student loans.

I was in the process of finishing my college degree at night for Computer Programming and things seemed to be on track, except I was still with Shaw. At this point, I remember wondering, "What's he still doing here?" He didn't have a job. I paid the bills and his mother paid his tuition to a part time technical college. As the kind of person who likes to take care of people, I was the perfect sucker for Shaw. If only I'd seen it then!

I came home one night and told Shaw our relationship wasn't working and I wanted him to leave. I really meant it and we broke up—but, he always conned his way back into my life. We went through this ritual for four years; breaking up, working things out, and then adding something new, like unfaithfulness and lies on his part. Eventually, I think, he beat me down as a person. Over the years, he eroded my self -worth until I believed I didn't deserve anyone better.

The last time Shaw came back, he wanted to get married. I told him he'd have to keep a job for at least one year and help pay our living expenses. Amazingly, he'd never done anything so difficult before. His mother had always bailed him out of everything,

What was I thinking?

***Sherry and
Codey
(1993)***

***Codey's Fourth
grade picture.
(2000)***

***Codey 8-years-
old on my mom
and stepfather's
boat.***

5

Sherry L. Pierce

**Sherry &
Codey (1995)**

**Sherry
(1999)**

**My house in
Kentucky.**

Chapter 2

We had a smooth eight or nine months. Shaw found a job and seemed to be trying to make our relationship work. My major soft spot was my 8-year-old son Codey. Shaw could always get to me when it came to Codey. They were buddies, and my son was close to Shaw. (Now I understand, why—Shaw himself had the mentality of an 8 year old!) I should've worried about Codey out-growing his buddy Shaw.

In June of 2000, I realized I was pregnant. I hadn't planned on having more children, but I was happy when I told Shaw, and he seemed pleased. In a moral sense I wanted to get married, but something told me not to. However, in Sept. 2000, we had a small ceremony at my house and became man and wife.

Sometimes I think I believed if I gave Shaw a normal family, which he never had, and a normal life, he would turn into a good husband and father.

One day in late September, I began having terrible cramps while at work. I went to the bathroom and passed a lot of blood. Certain I was having a miscarriage, I drove straight to my doctor's office, and he agreed that I was losing the baby. But after an ultrasound later that day, he gave me the good news that my baby was perfectly fine. The placenta (the sack that encloses the baby and provides nutrients) had a tear in it, called a placental abruption. No guarantees, but he ordered strict bed rest and we hoped for the best.

Although I planned to follow the doctor's advice, I was concerned about Codey, my job, and who would take care of everything around the house. I explained everything to Shaw and he promised to help. That lasted about one week. I had appointments with the obstetrician every week, so he could monitor the baby, but I couldn't even get Shaw to take me to the doctor's office.

My employer brought a laptop computer to my home and allowed me to work there at 100% pay, which was a huge weight off my shoulders. Unfortunately, I couldn't always take it easy, because I didn't get much cooperation from Shaw.

Sherry and mother Brinda at Gabriel's baby shower.

Chapter 3

I was weak and swollen toward the third trimester of pregnancy, and I never felt good. I made Shaw go to prenatal classes with me because he was a first time parent. During the movie at one of the classes, he started laughing and making fun of it. I was so ashamed of his immaturity.

I thought the time had come on the morning of March 18, 2000, when I started having contractions, so I called the doctor and he sent me to the emergency room. Shaw was more concerned about getting to Burger King for breakfast than with my problems, but that suited me fine. I felt less stress when he was out of the room. The doctor sent me home, saying it was false labor.

On March 22, I got virtually no sleep. I went to the bathroom around 5:30 am and saw blood. I called the doctor, who said he'd meet us at the hospital. Once we arrived at the hospital, I called my mother; Brinda and Shaw called his mother, Hagatha.

The doctor decided to go ahead and deliver the baby that day—a great relief to me.

Shaw was out of the room through most of my labor, either eating or smoking, but I had to put up with his loud, obnoxious, red-neck mother, a "wanna be" nurse who worked as a nurse's aide in a nearby hospital. When the nurses came in to ask me questions, she'd answer for me before I could even open my mouth.

By 11:30 am, I'd dilated to around 9 cm, and my mother asked me where Shaw was. Several people went looking for him. The doctor said, "This baby isn't going to wait." Shaw was so backward, he didn't even notice when he made his grand entrance that we'd all been waiting for him. The delivery was rough. All I can remember is Shaw's breath in my face telling me to push and repeating everything the doctor said. I finally told him to shut the f—k up and get out of my face. The doctor asked Shaw if he wanted to cut the cord and his reply was, "I would, but I just ate."

At that moment, I wished the doctor would had given me the damn scissors so I could jerk Shaw's tongue out of his mouth and cut it off. When the doctor held up my son, Gabriel Jacob, he was so tiny—unlike Codey, who was eight pounds, eleven ounces at birth. Gabriel weighed in at only six pounds, five ounces. Tiny and so beautiful.

The doctor passed him to a nurse, and she cleaned him while the doctor stitched me up. After a minute, I realized my baby Gabe wasn't crying. I asked if he was okay and the nurse said, "He's just quiet." They brought Gabe to me, wrapped in a warm blanket, and I touched my son for the first time. I felt relieved that he was healthy and all the struggle of the pregnancy was wiped from my mind. I was so proud.

Next, they prepped me for a tubal ligation, which I'd decided during my pregnancy was a good idea. The whole time I was trying to see my baby, Shaw was entertaining himself with my stepfather's camcorder, which he had no clue how to use.

When I awakened after surgery, they told me Gabriel was ready for his first meal. I breast-fed him, and this was my first chance to hold my sweet angel. Shaw had left the room, smoking an "It's a boy" cigar with his buddies. Codey stayed in the room with me. I wished time would stand still so I could savor this perfect moment, staring at this tiny black-haired baby with his perfect little nose and tiny fingers. I felt so complete with my two sons. At that moment, I knew I'd accomplished everything important that I needed to in life. Codey and I were so proud of our baby Gabe.

Chapter 4

The next day was a blur, because I was really swollen and didn't feel well; the doctor said it was just my hormones and fluid from the delivery. Shaw said he needed his sleep, so he went home for the night. I had a private hospital room, with an extra bed, so Codey stayed with me. Shaw was a person who required a lot of sleep. He'd taken the week off of work, so he didn't have to get up early, but the birth of the baby just wore him out.

The next day the nurses said I'd be discharged sometime that morning. I called Shaw at home and asked him to come get us. When the doctor stepped in, I showed him how swollen I was, especially my feet. I could hardly walk on them. He mentioned giving me a water pill that would help with the fluid retention, but he wanted to wait to see if the fluid would absorb itself because the medicine would also dry up my breast milk and it would prevent me from breastfeeding Gabriel. My doctor was very much in favor of breastfeeding. He said if the swelling didn't improve within a week or so, I should call his office. In the meantime, he advised me to keep my legs and feet elevated.

My doctor signed the discharge papers, but we still had to wait for the baby's pediatrician to come in and examine him so he could be discharged also. When Gabriel's doctor stopped in to chat with us, Shaw asked him, "When is check- out time?" As though we were in a motel.

Finally, we were able to leave the hospital, but Shaw wanted to stop at Steak & Shake on the way home, even though I told him I was exhausted and needed to prop up my legs. Codey was spending the weekend with his dad, so Shaw, the baby, and I had the house to ourselves. I just wanted to crawl into my warm bed and rest. That idea was quickly ruined by a Saturday night visit from the cast of the movie "Deliverance."

Shawn's mother, father, sister, aunt, uncle, brother-in-law, and niece descended on us for a surprise late night visit. I felt bad and wasn't prepared to handle a house full of people pawing at my newborn son. I stayed up as long as I could, and then used the excuse that I wanted to feed the baby in private, so we could lie down. When I went back to my bedroom to nurse Gabriel, I'll never forget the humiliation Shaw's mother put me through.

The baby had a little bit of trouble nursing when he was latching on to my nipple, a common thing for newborns. Hagatha followed me into the bedroom and wouldn't leave. She grabbed my breast and shoved it into my baby's mouth, telling me I wasn't doing it right. I felt like a cow. That was all I could take! I asked Shaw for help and told him I needed to be alone with the baby. His family left me alone, but they stayed for another two hours.

Later that night, I explained to Shaw what his mother had done. He always defended her and acted as if he didn't understand what she did wrong. The next morning at eight am Hagatha called. I answered the phone. Shaw was, of course, sleeping. Hagatha wanted to bring more of her family over again. That's when I drew the line. I made Shaw call her back and tell her no. He blamed it on me of course, but at that point, I didn't care. You see, in our whole relationship these people had absolutely nothing to do with me, except to cause trouble at any opportunity. When Gabriel was born they become sugary sweet, but I knew it wasn't real.

Shaw's mom was furious that we didn't let her come over, so she refused to speak to us for a week. This just killed Shaw, but I could not have been happier. Finally, a little peace—or so I thought!

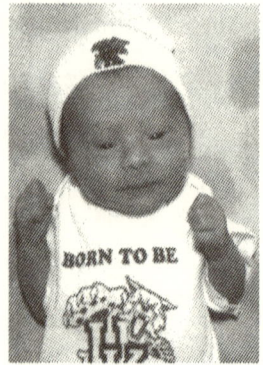

***Gabriel Jacob
at birth.***

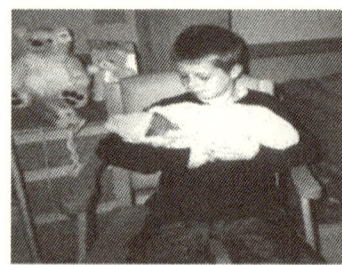

***Big brother
holding little
brother.***

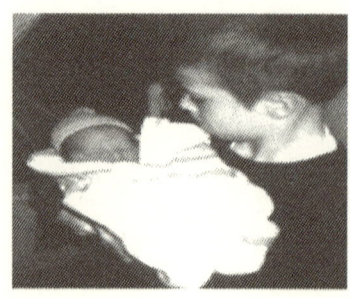

***My <u>sweet</u>
boys.***

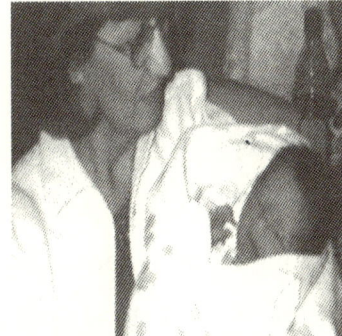

"Na Na"
holding Gabriel
at birth.

Sherry, Papaw Loyd,
Codey and Gabriel
getting ready for
hospital discharge.

Chapter 5

On March 29, I woke up with a headache that I cannot even begin to describe. Shaw was just going back to work and he was getting ready. I needed to get Codey up and ready for school. When I stood up, I felt sick and had to run to the bathroom to vomit. I told myself this was just a bad migraine headache. In the past, I'd get migraines around the time of my period. But this was on a different level of pain than my usual headaches. It felt like I had a snake moving around on the right side of my head. When I told Shaw how sick I was, he said to go lie down.

I remember Shaw leaving for work and, as time went on, the pain became almost unbearable. I had Gabriel in the bed with me. He was such an angel; he only cried when he needed to nurse. I would roll over to let him nurse, and then roll back to the side of the bed and vomit into a trashcan. I looked up at the clock and knew Codey would be home from school soon, and I needed to unlock the front door for him so he could get in the house.

When I tried to get out of bed, my legs crumpled and I collapsed to the floor. For some reason, I couldn't get up. My body felt totally numb. I remember wondering why I felt that way. How could I get to the door? I crawled out of my room, down the hallway, and unlocked the front door. Somehow, I made it back to my room.

I don't remember hearing Codey come in, but I do recall him shaking me and asking me if I was okay. He had a worried look on his face. He touched my cheek and said, "Mom what's wrong with your face?"

He brought me a wet washcloth to put on my forehead. I knew I needed help, but I couldn't think clearly, and one of my arms wouldn't move.

I told Codey to get me the phone, and I paged my mother.

Mom called me right back and I told her something was wrong and I needed her. This probably scared my mother, because it wasn't something I would normally say. She lived about two miles down the road, so she arrived at my house within minutes.

When she came in, she looked at me and asked me what was wrong. I remember telling her I needed to go to the hospital. I told her to call 911. I got frustrated with her because she kept trying to get me dressed. I had on boxer shorts and a nursing bra. She tried to help me up, but I slid off the bed. "Have you taken anything?" She asked. I said no and kept pleading with her to call 911. She struggled to put my housecoat on me, but my arm wouldn't go into the hole.

I finally screamed at her, "Do you want me to die?" If we don't get some help, I'll die." At this point, I was terrified, because my speech was slurred and I felt I was losing control of everything. I grabbed the phone from my mother and dialed 911.

The ambulance seemed to take forever. I heard the siren from a distance, moving closer to our house. When they arrived, they asked if I'd taken any medications. Because of my age, they assumed I'd taken some drug and was having side effects. (I don't think there's room in the medical field for assumptions.)

During the ride to the hospital, I lapsed in and out of consciousness, but I remember the EMS worker taking my blood pressure and when she got the reading, she exclaimed, "Oh, my GOD!" That was real comforting!

My next memories are fragmented. I recall a young doctor with long hair, who said, "We're going to give you a little something for your headache." Then I felt my head slam down on the table.

I found out later I'd had a Grand Mal seizure in the emergency room, and then a second one when they sent me for my first CAT scan. Mom said it seemed like forever before anyone came out to talk with her. She was worried because the baby was getting hungry. She finally asked a nurse if I could please nurse the baby. Mom had called Shaw but he hadn't arrived yet. The doctor approached my mother. He said, "We're making arrangements for someone from the nursery to bring formula for the baby. Sherry has suffered a stroke, and she won't be able to continue nursing the baby because of her medication." He touched her arm, offering comfort. "We've called two of the best neurosurgeons and neurologists in the state."

Mom said she was in shock and didn't know what to say. About that time, my stepfather David and Shaw came through the emergency doors. Shaw immediately began calling his family.

A couple of hours later a doctor came out and introduced himself as Dr. Horn, a neurosurgeon. He explained that I'd suffered a hemorrhage on the right side of my brain and a blood clot had formed on the left side. I was on medication to reduce the swelling in my brain and to thin my blood and keep it from clotting. They'd also given me a medicine called Dilantin to prevent further seizures. The conversation was directed to Shaw at first, but he showed little interest and didn't seem to understand what was happening. After that, the doctors directed their words to my mother and stepfather. When the doctors left the room, my mother and stepfather looked at each other at the same time and said, "Shaw hasn't got a clue!"

My mother attempted to call my father, but couldn't reach him, because he worked night shifts.

Shaw said he'd call him. When I talk to my dad about this, he still gets very emotional and upset. He said Shaw called him at work and bluntly said, "Loyd, you need to get to the hospital. Sherry has blood clots all over her brain and stuff! "

Dad later said, "That idiot had me so upset and confused, I didn't even tell the boss I was leaving."

The doctors told my family they'd do another CAT scan later. When they ran the second scan, they said the clot was larger and I had only a 30% chance of living; if it continued to grow, they would have to surgically remove the clot. They needed Shaw to sign a release form for a possibly dangerous dye test that would provide a better image of what was going on inside my brain.

Mom said through a lot of the testing and waiting she was concerned about the way Shaw reacted. She said he was in and out of the hospital. He would go out to eat with guys from work and his family. She wondered, *how can he eat at a time like this?*

She said her real concern was that when the doctors would come in and talk to the family, most of the time

Shaw wasn't even there. When they needed his signature for the test, his family had to go find him. He sat there and would not sign the papers. He'd shown no emotion through the whole ordeal, but now when we really needed something from him, he was trying for an Oscar. His mother consoled him saying, *"It must be so hard for you, Shaw"*

Later that night my mother was surprised when Shaw asked where he could find my car keys and purse. Mom had driven my car to the hospital when I had the stroke, because the baby seat was already in it. She gave him the keys and my purse—after all, he was my husband. During the whole hospital stay, he left his junky Ford Tempo that his mother had given him in the hospital parking lot and drove my Honda Prelude. Because of his driving record, I never let him drive my car. Mom knew I would have had a fit if I knew he was driving my car.

I was told later that as I moved in and out of consciousness, I often asked for my kids. I told my dad not to tell my grandmother Marian, who was in her 80's, that I was sick. I was so worried that they'd go tell my Grandma that her "Sherry baby" was sick, and it would upset her.

My grandmother is my wisdom; in my eyes she can do nothing wrong. A visit with her is an antidote to life's trials and tribulations. Truly, a day spent with her drinking coffee and eating her fresh baked banana nut bread and listening to the stories of the old days (I've heard them a dozen times but every time feels like the first) is a day in paradise for me.

They did tell my grandmother, and even brought her to see me, but thank the Lord, I don't remember.

My next memory is being wheeled on a table down a corridor and looking over into a waiting room area. I saw my friends, people I worked with, my cousins, and other family members. I thought I was having a weird dream. Some man was speaking next to my ear for about twenty minutes, nothing but gibberish. I couldn't process or understand anything he was saying. I thought, *Good GOD, when is this guy gonna be done with this mumbling?* He seemed so sincere, but he was getting on my nerves. I thought *He sure smells good.*

The one thing he did say that I understood was that they were taking care of me. That made me feel good.

I believe I lost almost two days until my next memory. I looked up and saw my cousin Kenny and my brother Duane standing beside my bed. This seemed strange, because I hadn't seen Kenny for six years, and my brother lived in Louisiana, twelve or thirteen hours away. I knew at that moment something awful had happened to me. Normally complete bullshiters, they both had such serious faces. I started crying, because it was the first time in this confusion that I'd felt a sense of peace.

Because of life's changes, I'd lost touch with Kenny, but he was still very dear to me. My brother Duane is my Wayney. When we were, little I called him "Wayney" and he called me "Snibby."

That night, he touched my hand and said "Its okay, Snibby."

Chapter 6

My next memory was of me asking my mother what was wrong with me, and wanting to see my kids.

I don't really remember what my mother said was wrong, but she did make sure the baby was brought in. My son Codey came in with his father, Chris. I remember wanting to hold the baby, but the Nurses wouldn't let me.

A dark- haired, nice looking young doctor entered the room shortly after my kids left and said, "Hello, Sherry. My name is Doctor Horn. Do you remember me?"

I said yes, but I really didn't, later I found out Dr. Horn was the *good smelling* doctor speaking all the gibberish in my ear. As I slipped in and out of my consciousness, I kept asking everybody what was wrong with me. My family had finally asked Dr. Horn to please stop by and explain my condition.

I asked, "What kind of doctor are you?"

He replied, "A Neurosurgeon."

I thought to myself, *what kind of doctor did he say he was?*

He said, "Do you know why you're here?"

I said, "Yes, I had a really bad headache."

He smiled a warm smile and said, "Yes, you sure did. As a result of your bad headache, you suffered a hemorrhagic stroke."

My first thought was, this *guy is nuts, I'm way too young for a stroke.* At this point, I just played along with what I thought was bullshit. It seemed like everyone but me was crazy, and I knew that somehow I had to get to the bottom of all this. Dr. Horn went on to say, "We're still running tests and trying to find out the extent of the damage."

The whole time I'm thinking, Ok *weirdo, I am here talking to you. I'm obviously fine.* I didn't know that a stroke was a brain injury, or the physical and cognitive effects that go along with one.

He said, "We do know you have full left- sided paralysis."

I asked, "What do you mean?"

He said, "You're paralyzed on your left side." I looked at my left hand and tried to move it, but nothing happened. I immediately started crying, not really because I was sad about the paralysis, but because I just had no control over my emotions. I thought to myself that I would try really hard when he left the room, and I would move everything and show everyone I was fine. I was in major denial for a couple of days.

They moved me from the ICU to a private room on the Transitional Care Unit, which provides a less extensive level of care than ICU. Strangely, through the first three or four days, I have no memory of Shaw. I didn't ask to see him and do not really know why. After I was settled into the private room, my doctors came in and said they were arranging for my husband and baby to stay in the room with me overnight. They were very concerned about me bonding with Gabriel.

That night, I woke up to hear the baby screaming. I looked around. Shaw was sleeping on a cot with Gabriel in a bassinette at his feet. For a minute, I almost forgot my condition and tried to get up. I couldn't move. I felt so helpless and incomplete. I couldn't get to my own baby.

Twice, I screamed at Shaw to get up. He didn't move. There was a wheeled table right beside Shaw's head with a pitcher of water on it. I took my right leg and kicked that sucker hard. The water went all over his head and the table turned over. Shaw screamed "what the f—k"... as he was wiping the water from his eyes.

A nurse ran in, asking what had happened. Shaw said I was acting crazy and violent. At that point, I didn't realize the fight I had ahead of me; against his lying, to make up for his shortcomings and his lazy, ignorant ways. I didn't say anything when the nurse was in the room but after she left, I looked at Shaw and said with all the strength I had, "If you don't wake your lazy fat ass up again for my baby, I'll show you what "crazy and violent" is!" He didn't say a word.

Chapter 7

I remember lying in my room and just wanting to see my mom. I asked a nurse if she could get my mother, and found out later that when they called up to the waiting room, Hagatha answered the phone. They said, "Sherry wants to see her mother." Although my mom was sitting right there in the room, Hagatha said "Okay," hung up the phone, and came to the room herself. When I saw her, I said to the nurse, "This is not my mother."

Hagatha said, "Her mother is sleeping." (My mother was awake). The nurse asked her to leave because I was getting really upset. I began to realize that before, I was always in control of my family, my life, and myself. There was no way this controlling, uneducated, hick bitch could have ever pried her way into my world then.

She was so damn mean that when she was sleeping, she had to keep one eye open to keep from killing herself! Now that I was out of commission, Hagatha thought she could easily take control. When I saw my mother next, I immediately asked, "Who's taking care of the baby?"

She replied, "Hagatha, and then went on to say, "We've been very concerned about the way she is acting with the baby, but we don't want to upset you. She announced today that no one is to hold the baby but her." Shaw's family also told my mom that the baby didn't need to be in the hospital 24 hours a day and they were going to take him home.

I told my mom, "No matter what, don't let her take the baby home with her." I pretty much made this clear to everyone. I knew Shaw was too weak and cowardly to stand up against his mother, so I told the doctor I wanted my baby with me. He had a talk with the family and said that under no circumstances should I become upset, so they should try to make me happy and comfortable. That's the only thing that kept them from taking my baby. Every time they'd say something about taking the baby, bless my mothers heart; she'd say, "We do not want to upset Sherry."

Shaw even approached my mother one night and said, "How would Sherry know if my mother took

Gabriel home?" My mother said, "You might lie to my daughter but your not going to get me to lie to her."

Doctor Horn came in to talk with me often He would always ask me what his name was. When you suffer a stroke, sometimes your short-term or long-term memory can be affected. I knew his name was a four-letter word, so I started calling him "Dr. Fart". Your emotions are also affected. One minute you may be crying, and the next laughing hysterically. When I would call him Dr. Fart, not only would it embarrass my family, but also I thought it was the funniest thing I'd ever said *every time I said it*. Thank GOD for Dr. Horn's sense of humor. He told me one time that only I could call him Dr. Fart.... He'd let it slide, considering everything I'd gone through.

Dr. Horn "Fart". (I still think it's funny!) Said I'd be transferred to a Rehabilitation Center for extensive in-patient therapy.

My last memory of the hospital was in my room with my mother, my brother Duane, my dad Loyd, step-grandmother Ann, my boss Lynne, cousin Trish, Hagatha, and Shaw's brother Caine. I didn't even know Caine, but all of the sudden he was there every day, supporting his poor sick sister-in-law. Come to find out he was staying at my house running up my phone bill. Tension was high between the families and the air was thick with it. I didn't know at the time what started the huge outburst, but my mother and father were yelling. Then Hagatha joined in, and out of nowhere Caine got involved. I remember Duane telling everyone to, "Stop! Please think about Sherry."

My parents' divorce thirteen years ago had been rough, but they should have had enough sense to know I didn't need any extra stress at that point. I think my illness and the circus sideshow of my husband and in-laws just took a toll on everybody.

I found out later that the fight was about the previous night. One of the Nurses had left my bedrail down, and I turned over and fell out of the bed. Shaw was at home. He stopped staying with me after *"I got all violent" and kicked his ass with a pitcher of water.* The hospital called Shaw and told him I had fallen out of bed and that they were sending me for x-rays to make sure I didn't break anything.

Really concerned, I'm sure, he went back to sleep. Later that morning my mother came up to the hospital and they told her what had happened. My mother is a little woman, but she's very feisty. It really pissed her off that Shaw didn't go to the hospital right away or call her. He claimed I called him after the hospital did and told him not to worry and to not come up there.

I know I was suffering from a brain injury and all, but you don't have to be a "rocket scientist" to figure out he was full of shit! After falling, I was immediately taken to be x-rayed. I don't think I had a cell phone stuck up my ass to call him with. I'm not sure what my dad had to do with it, but my mom was pissed at him also. She felt he was standing up for Shaw, and not really seeing what was going on around him.

She probably wasn't too far off on that one. Dad's main concern was his baby girl; I was always a "Daddy's girl". He just wanted to keep the peace. He told me later that he thought Shaw was just young and didn't know what to do. (Needless to say, dad's opinion has changed since this happened).

They put me in an ambulance and drove me downtown to the rehab facility. When I first arrived, I had no idea what was ahead of me. I remember being really scared because it looked like a nursing home with a lot of old people in wheelchairs. My first thought was, *"My GOD, will I have to be here 'til I get old? Is this it for me?"* I started sobbing. My family was very upset; they were not used to me having emotional outbursts, and I felt sorry they had to see me this way.

A woman named Denise introduced herself and said she would be my caseworker. Shaw was lying on the bed next to me. He put his feet up and asked, "Where's the nursery that watches the baby?" I have no idea what gave him the idea these people were going to take care of the baby, but she set him straight in a hurry.

She said, "Sir, we are giving your wife a private room only because her doctors requested it because of the extenuating circumstances and how important it is for her to bond with the baby. We don't have a nursery here, but we *highly recommend* that you stay here with the baby and promote their bonding."

I think reality hit Shaw right square in the face. I'm sure he was thinking, *Oh shit, we are at a point where somebody's expecting me to do something!*

Later, I heard Shaw on the phone talking to a friend. He said, "Oh no, she didn't have a stroke. Only old people have strokes!"

I thought to myself…*How can he be here for me when he doesn't even know or accept what happened to me?* The first night, Shaw said he was tired and wanted to go home and get some sleep. He would have let me make *any* decision about the baby at that point because he just wanted to get out of there. I told him, "Fine. I want my mother to take the baby with her."

Sherry L. Pierce

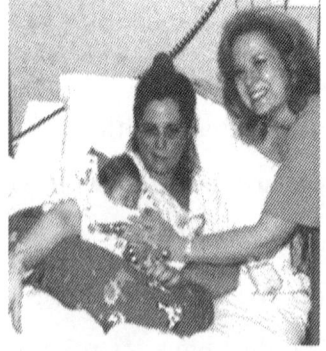

Sherry and Gabriel in TCU with a wonderful nurse named—Tracy.

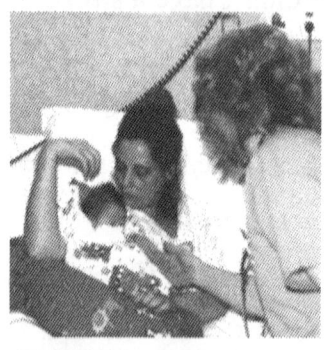

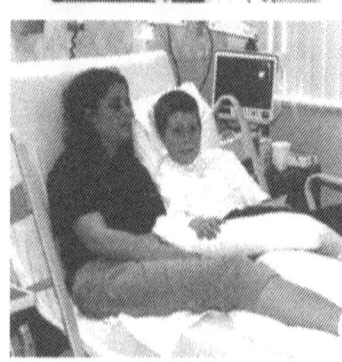

Sherry and Codey Easter Sunday in Rehab facility.

Sherry, Codey and Gabriel in Rehab facility.

Codey Easter Sunday in Rehab facility.

Chapter 8

My therapy started early the next day, a nurse's aide named Angie came in the morning and explained my schedule. I had occupational therapy first, then speech therapy. After that, I'd return to my room for lunch, then go to physical therapy. I had no clue what this girl was talking about, but I liked her! She was down to earth, and she didn't look as though she pitied me or felt sorry for me (which I hated). She had Shaw's number the first second she met him. Angie became my friend and confidante.

When you go to a rehab facility, any modesty you had goes away immediately! Total strangers wipe your ass, bathe you, dress you, and witness the weakest moments of your life. If you are having a *"pity party"*, these people do not want to be invited. If they see any bullshit or lack of support from family members, they have no problem stepping in. I have a special kind of respect for therapists and people who care for and motivate the disabled. It takes a unique kind of person to deal with this stress day in and day out. You would definitely have to love your job to be able to survive.

Angie helped me sit up and tied a ("Gait Belt") around my waist. She then brought me to the edge of the bed. "On the count of three, you're going to stand, pivot, and transfer to the wheelchair. I have you. One, two, three."

I tried to stand, but my left leg collapsed and my left arm fell off the bed and dangled at my side like dead weight. I looked at her and said, "That sucked."…

She laughed, and said, "We'll get better, but you have to watch your arm. You can't let it flop like that or you could hurt it." Therefore, I started calling my arm "Lucy" because it flopped around loosely all the time. I treated it as if it was a baby so I could remember to take care of it. I had no feeling in my entire left side, so it would have been very easy to injure myself, as I could not feel the sensation of pain.

Angie wheeled me to an elevator to go to occupational therapy. An old man who'd also suffered a stroke looked at me and started screaming, "Her too young! Her too young!"

I regret to admit that I'd never allowed religion or prayer to influence my life. However, right then I prayed, "GOD, please get me through this tragedy." After the encounter with the old man, I just wanted to go back to bed, but they wouldn't let me.

The occupational therapists 's name was Pam, and she seemed nice. She said she was going to involve Gabriel in my therapy. That sounded good to me. "I thought to myself, *Then I can go home and everything will be okay.*"

She said, "First, I'm going to show you how to dress." Right then I realized, *These people are getting me prepared to live the rest of my life like this.* In my mind, I refused to accept that! Through the rest of our session, I got increasingly depressed. She finally said, "I think that's enough for today. I'm going to take you to speech therapy."

My Speech Therapist's name was Tammy Pierce. I automatically liked her because she shared my maiden name. She was very nice, but at first, I felt liiike shhhe waaas taaalkiiiing verry sloooooow to me. This totally offended me, because it made me feel stupid. Now I realize she was just feeling me out, to see the extent of my cognitive damage. This damage affects short and long-term memory, speech, problem solving, reasoning skills, time management, and your patience level. Pretty much everything you need mentally to function in this world.

The first couple of things she did were gravy...She would give me a word, then ask me a couple of questions, then go back and ask me what the word was. I thought to myself then, *I do not want these people to think I'm crazy, so I have to do well on this stuff.* I decided I'd remember everyone's name, all my medications, and everything about my therapy and the stroke that I possibly could. The bad thing was that my mind still felt hazy most of the time. I was not myself. I almost felt like my brain was on vacation. I decided to use a method called word association.

I took a class in it through my employment about five years ago. About sixty people attended the class, and the instructor met everyone as they entered the classroom. He asked their names and whom they worked for. Throughout that whole day, the man would call on different people throughout the room. He remembered every person's name and whom they worked for. He impressed me. I used the technique to remember phone numbers, study for exams in college, and for work related situations.

However, I had no idea then that I would someday need what I learned in an eight-hour seminar at such a critical time in my life. I think I impressed the pants off Tammy. In a way, I felt like I was cheating. but I got through her session with ease. Tammy told me my assertiveness would be an asset to me in my recovery.

Tammy took me to lunch. After lunch, Angie came to get me for physical therapy. A nice young man swiftly walked up to me and said, "My name is Mike Shircliff". He took me to a mat and immediately started exercising my left leg. I liked that.... I felt we were accomplishing something.

I asked, "Can I be blunt?"

He said, "Yes."

"I don't want a bunch of bullshit, Will I walk again?"

He said, "First of all, I'll make you a promise; I will never bullshit you! You give me everything you have… I will work you hard and you will walk." From there on out, he was my GOD!

I was extremely tired when they finally returned me to my room. Shaw had not been there yet, but my mother had brought Codey and Gabriel. I was worried about Codey. He acted different, a little distant. It all of the sudden hit me. *"What is he feeling?" "How is this affecting him?" "My poor sweet Codey."* He was alternately staying with my mother and with his dad, Chris, and stepmother, Michele. They were so supportive through everything. When I needed Codey, they made sure he was there. I was very lucky to have Chris and Michele, who were so thoughtful and caring through all my trials.

I remember trying to put my hair back in a ponytail one night. Michele sat in my hospital bed with me and French-braided my hair. That, some people may say, is

not normal. But it felt normal to me...she is my true
friend.

Chapter 9

When I told Mom that my therapists were going to involve the baby in my daily routine, I could see her concern; how would the baby get there. My mother was going to have to go back to work, and by this time, she obviously knew I couldn't depend on Shaw.

Later that day a psychologist named Susan Berry came in. She explained that sometimes people who go through brain injuries, paralysis, and childbirth might need someone to talk with about their feelings. She recommended going on an anti-depressant, I automatically refused; being the type of person who believed you should work through your own shit yourself. I was never interested in that "psycho-babble bullshit" or taking drugs to change the way things are supposed to go naturally. At the time, I didn't realize that nothing about this stroke was natural and it was changing everything. The way I perceived things, my sense of humor, and my moods.

You take a compulsive perfectionist, give her a stroke that affects perception, mobility, and emotions and what do you get ? A restrained, slowed- down person who cannot even distinguish what the hell anything is anymore, and can't help but cry about it.

Shaw came up that night. He didn't say much about the baby, which suited me fine because I knew Gabriel was safe with my mother. I asked Shaw to please go pay our taxes. We'd had our taxes prepared at a service right before I delivered Gabriel, and I knew we owed the government $320.00. He also brought some mail and my child support check for Codey. I signed it and told him to deposit it and withdraw enough money to pay the taxes.

The bank account was in my name only. I never had Shaw's name added because he wasn't a real big contributor. I always took care of everything anyway. My employment check was deposited directly into my account. Shaw had returned to work and received at least three paychecks since all of this had started, but I have no idea where that money went!

I gave him, the utility bills and the cable TV bill. I told him to get my bank card from my purse and take enough money to pay those bills, and I'd figure out the rest later. I was starting to get a really bad headache. (Just thinking about him being in control of the money made me sick). When he got my purse he said, "Oh, your bank card isn't in your purse. I have it."

I said, "Why do you have it?"

He said, "When you were in the hospital, I needed $20.00 for spending money, so I went to the money machine."

I asked , "Shaw, how much have you taken since then?"

He said, "None. I swear." (*"I did not have sexual relations with that woman, Monica Lewinsky" – Bill Clinton)* This is a guy who has the memory span of a two- year- old. I think I may have sent him with my bank card to withdraw money twice, the whole time we were together. Nevertheless, he managed to remember my four-digit pin number. Isn't that convenient?

After he left, the more I thought about it, the more suspicious I became. The next morning, I told my doctor I needed an hour to conduct some personal business. I decided I wasn't going to tell anybody what

I was thinking…I was actually hoping my mind was playing tricks on me, or my newfound paranoia had gotten the best of me. I asked Angie if they had a fax machine at the nurse's desk. She said, "Yes." Then I called the bank and asked if they could fax me some information. After I faxed them a written consent, they sent a copy of all the activity on my account since March 29th (the day of the stroke).

There were fifteen withdraws and zero deposits, except for my automatic deposits. I highlighted the dates and the amounts, and totaled them at the bottom. I was missing $900.00!. I went through the rest of the day without telling anyone.

When I finished therapy and went to lunch, I called Shaw. I asked him if he'd paid the three bills and the taxes. He said, "Yes." I asked if he'd be coming by later, and he said he would.

I then called the tax service and asked if Shaw had paid the taxes. He had not. I called the cable and utility companies, and was not surprised to hear they hadn't been paid either.

I was so upset. My first thought was, *I'm going to kill this lying thieving bastard.* Then I thought, *This can't be right. I'm going to approach this calmly. I have the fax and I'll give him a chance to explain.* When Shaw came in that night, I handed the fax to him and said, "Can you explain this to me?"

Of course, he took forever examining it. Then he looked up at me, wadded up the paper, threw it on the bed, and said, "You slow retard. You are so stupid."

About that time, Angie walked in and asked, "Sherry, is everything okay?"

I told her yes and started to cry....

She said, " Are you about ready for your shower?" She helped me into the wheelchair and wheeled me over to the sink so I could brush my teeth. I asked her to give us a minute before she wheeled me down to the showers. She hesitantly left the room. (Later Angie told me that she heard him call me a slow retard...that's why she entered the room when she did.)

I asked Shaw, "How could you do something like this?" I demanded.

He said, "You have it all confused."

Right then, I lost it. I called him a thief and who knows what else. I was so upset! I'm not sure what I was doing, but they say that sometimes new stroke patients forget their deficits. I started to get up and fell out of the chair onto the floor. Shaw looked down at me for what seemed like an eternity. He just smiled and walked straight out of the room and left the building. Angie ran in with two nurses and they helped me up. They'd seen Shaw leave and were totally disgusted that he didn't help me.

Forget everything else... what kind of man steals from his wife and kids when she is on her deathbed? What kind of man calls his wife a *"slow retard"* after she suffers a stroke, due to the delivery of *his* child? And lastly, what kind of a man, no matter what his wife was saying, watches her paralyzed body fall to the floor and leave her there? I asked myself all of these questions and came to the same conclusion that any *sane* person would reach (You heard me, I said *sane person) I* did not want to be with him ever again! I was done!!!!

As if that night wasn't long enough, about an hour later the phone rang in my room. It was my stepfather, David. He said, "Sherry, what's happened?"

"Why ?" I asked

"Shaw called and said you had some kind of spell. He thinks maybe you've had another stroke." My stepfather said his first question to Shaw had been, "Where are you?"

Shaw had said, "At home."

My stepfather then asked , "Did you tell a doctor?"

"No."

My stepfather said, "You think she's having a spell, but you didn't bother to tell anyone at the hospital?"

My stepfather and mother agreed then that Shaw was up to something. I explained everything to my family and showed them the faxes as proof It really upset them that he had the nerve to call and scare the hell out of them, trying to make it look like I'd lost it, just to cover up his lies and immoral actions.

I said, "I bet he wishes I *had* suffered another stroke. Maybe it would get my damn memory this time and I wouldn't remember what he did."

Chapter 10

The next day I was in my room with my mother and my cousin Trish. (Trish had been so supportive since the stroke.... she was there for me every day, helping me with business and just being there to talk when I needed to bend an ear.) My mother had decided to take a family leave of absence from her work so she could be there for the kids and me when I came home.

We were just talking when the phone rang. It was Hagatha. She started by saying that I had no clue what it was like for her family to come to the hospital and see me in the shape I was in!

I said, "It must be awful!"

She then said, "You make matters worse by accusing my son of being a thief! Have you lost your mind?" Before I could get anything out, she started having a one- sided conversation with herself. "So you're saying you don't want me, Buck (Shaw's father), or my kids to come see you anymore?" Obviously, Shaw & Buck were there with her, and she was adding her own drama to the mix of things.

I replied, "Who had the stroke here, woman? I *didn't* say that, but now that I mention it, it would have been a pretty good comeback!" I hung up on her. I will have to agree with my stepfather. He said that Hagatha is right out of the movie "Throw Momma From the Train." Big mouth, greasy head, cowardly son and all!

Five days passed and Shaw didn't come to see me. My therapists were getting concerned about the lack of support on his behalf and were wondering what would happen when I returned home. He did call one time and asked, "What's your problem?"

I said, "You're working against me, Shaw. You're not here for me."

"I don't know how to be! Teach me."

I said, "This is not something you can teach. You can't teach compassion and support for a family member. It's in your raising; it's what you're born with." I truly believe that statement from him was probably the last honest statement I would ever receive from his dumb ass.

Because I know… "Throw Momma From the Train" sure didn't teach him anything in his childhood except how to connive and deceive people.

When Shaw was sixteen, Hagatha put him in a facility for disturbed kids because she couldn't handle him anymore. When he and his siblings were babies and she needed a break from being a mom, she'd give the kids to family members. Shaw was given to his grandpa when he was a baby.

She must have been on some kind of mean drunk when she named her two girls. She named one Militia and the other after an alcoholic beverage, Margarita. She is a walking dysfunction.

I'm not making excuses for Shaw's actions by any means; I've always felt there comes a time when an adult has to answer for their own actions. Blaming your actions on parents is cowardly. Everyone should know there is a difference between right and wrong.

I heard a saying once, "When you see a snake, never mind where he came from." In Shaw's case, he isn't the sharpest tool in the shed to begin with.

My cousin Tomeika met one of Shaw's co-workers, Ed Haskell, when I was in the hospital and started dating him. This would be a blessing because if I knew anything, I knew Shaw always had trouble keeping the least bit of "drama" to himself. I knew I could get information about what Shaw was up to through Ed and my cousin.

Tomeika told me that Shaw told Ed, he and Militia (a very fitting name for her) went to see a lawyer about divorcing me. The lawyer supposedly told Shaw it would look terrible if he started divorce proceedings while his wife was in the hospital after suffering a stroke. He also told him he'd better contribute some money for the baby and get involved somehow in what was going on with the baby and my therapy. (That was a joke; I thought, "contribute." Shaw only understood the word "withdraw").

Militia had a problem with me from the first time we met. She's one of those rough- necks stuck in the early 80's, with the feathered bangs, bright blue eye shadow, and a bad perm. One of those bitches that has a problem with any woman who is the least bit educated or attractive. She is the goddamn bully at school who would be smoking in the bathroom when you walked in and threaten you with your life if you told. Then for the next three years, she'd bump you in the hallway and rip your pictures of Duran Duran out of your locker. What did you do to deserve this treatment? Nothing! Nothing but exist, be somewhat popular and pretty, and have a cute boyfriend. My bully in school was Stephanie; Militia was just like her. But I have grown up since my school days, and she did not intimidate me a bit.

Over the last couple of years, she concocted a reason to hate me. She dated a guy who was a big, red-headed, ugly drughead . When they broke up, Shaw and I were having one of our many fights and I went out with some co-workers. That night I saw her boyfriend. He was obviously interested in me, but I was definitely not interested in him!

"Big ugly dude" must have told Militia he saw me. Presto!…she could finally say she hated me because supposedly I wanted her man. As if I really cared

whether she liked me or not. She never gave me a chance in the first place!

I always questioned in my mind her special closeness to Shaw (A little on the freaky side if you ask me!) One night when I was at the rehab hospital, I called my house to talk to Shaw. He answered the phone, and then she picked up. I said, "Was that Militia?"

He said, "Yes."

"What's she doing there?"

"Well, I really just didn't want to be alone."

I said, "Where is she?"

"She's sleeping in our bed and I'm on the couch."

That was weird. I did not want that bitch in my bed. I mean, wasn't it strange? This is the bitch that told Hagatha the previous Thanksgiving that if I came to their dinner, she'd "kick my ass." Hagatha ended up telling us she wasn't going to cook. We found out later from Margarita that she did indeed cook. We just weren't invited.

Ed also told Tomeika that Shaw was only working half a day every day, so he could come and help with my therapy. The interesting part about that was—neither my therapist nor I ever saw the lying bastard.

Shit was really getting deep and I began to wonder, *How can I get better with all of this craziness around me?* Therapy with the baby was going well. I'd learned how to change his diaper with one hand, how to dress him, and how to make his bottles. (The little socks were a bitch though!) The baby and I became the main attraction in the therapy room. The other patients started calling me "the lady with the baby". At first it bothered me, because I felt like we were on display, but as time went on I sensed these people enjoyed seeing Gabriel . It brightened their day.

Susan Berry (my psychologist) came to see me one evening. She said she'd been trying to get in touch with Shaw for two days, but he hadn't returned her phone calls. She wanted to talk with him about me going home, and find out what his plans were for the baby and me.

The next night, Susan came to my room and told me that she met with Shaw that afternoon. She said,

"Sherry, I talked with Shaw today, and he said he's not sure what he's going to do."

I said, "Susan, I'm strong enough for you to just be frank. Tell me your opinion of your conversation with him."

"Okay. In thirty minutes time, I figured out that he isn't capable of loving anybody. He has no clue, nor cares to get a clue, about what happened to you or what you're going through. His big question of the day, and probably every day, is "What about Shaw?"

I truly believe that her blunt response came from an intense concern for my well-being in case I decided to go home to the bastard.

Right then, I told my mom and stepfather, "I have to do something." The next day, Tomeika told me that Shaw had been going out to the bars with his sister and friends, partying himself to death. I continued to pay the bills from the hospital, while this loser was living in my house, driving my car, and partying his ass off on my dollar.

Later that day, I'd stopped answering the phone because Shaw and his coworkers were calling from his job and harassing me. When I would answer the phone, they'd say "Ms., will you walk over to the next room and get so and so?" I guess that was supposed to be funny because I couldn't walk. I started believing they were trying to drive me crazy! Sometimes they'd call and tell me Shaw was at work, puking sick, because of the pain he was experiencing by not having me in his life. I could hear people laughing in the background.

Please keep in mind; these are not highly- educated people by any means. Shaw worked at a quick oil-changing shop. Most of the employees were young punks or convicted felons. One of his pals, "Truck", was recently released from prison for armed robbery.

Shaw would call the nurse's desk and have them come and tell me that Codey or my dad was on the phone. When I took the call he said, "You better straighten up, or I'll just go downtown and get temporary custody of Gabriel, because you're not physically or mentally capable of taking care of him. You need to stop listening to everybody else, and keep your mouth shut. Stop accusing me of stealing and who knows what else, or you'll lose Gabriel. Have fun paying all my credit cards." (He had eight or nine credit cards from before our marriage that were maxed out). I was not scared. I knew he was too stupid to know about temporary custody on his own. He was getting some legal counsel, and his big mouth had let it slip. Nevertheless, his thought that I would pay off his credit card debt was a little ridiculous. (Maybe his lawyer was a "slow retard"!)

I needed to make a plan…. I had to hit him first. I knew he was too big of a loser and procrastinator to do anything just yet. He thought there was still a chance he could scare me into keeping my mouth shut and continue getting a **free ride**. I also knew I needed to get the temporary custody first, because it's harder to get it away from someone once it's been granted.

I needed a lawyer in a big way!!!!!

I had been keeping Angie updated on what was going on, and my doctors and therapists as well. The rehab facility staff was very supportive of my decision to divorce Shaw. They said they would be so worried about me if I decided to go home with him. They gave me names of several lawyers. I called a couple of them, and ran across one who caught my attention because he'd been a patient at my rehab facility when he broke his back due to a fall. He also had to learn how to walk again.

I wanted *him*. I thought, *This guy has been where I'm at right now.* As soon as I called him and gave him a breakdown of the situation, he was there within an hour.

He walked with a slight shuffle. He was very distinguished and professional- looking. His name was Brice Bolton. He sat and talked with my parents and I. He asked, "Sherry, are you sure you understand that getting this divorce is permanent?"

My answer was, "Mr. Bolton, I have experienced a life-altering situation. My Husband made a vow to stay by my side through sickness and in health. He has not only abandoned the baby and I, he has kicked me several times while I'm down. I know what I'm doing".

That very day Brice came back to the rehab facility with a divorce decree, temporary custody papers for Gabriel, a "no contact" motion (for Shaw to stay away from the hospital and stop the harassing phone calls), and a motion freezing all assets (to stop Shaw from running up any more debt). He also talked to the hospital security staff and made sure they wouldn't allow Shaw near me. You can't get any better than that!

That night, in the middle of the night, I had my dad and uncle take my spare car keys and move my car to Dad's house.

The next morning I called a locksmith and had all the locks changed on my house. I knew I had to get all of this shit done before Shaw was served, so he wouldn't have a chance to clean me out.

I called the bank and talked with the woman who'd faxed me the account information. She said Shaw came to the bank a few days before and tried to tell them his wife was in a mental institution. He showed them our marriage license and wanted to clean out the account. Thank GOD, she already knew what was going on. They told him they couldn't do anything because his name wasn't on the account. I went ahead and closed it so he wouldn't find a way to get to my money.

Chapter 11

Shaw came home from work that day and found his key wouldn't fit in the door. The strange thing is, he should've known something was happening because my car was missing from the driveway when the dumb ass left for work. He never bothered to call me to ask me where it was or to tell me it was gone.

I had a neighbor, who happened to be a police officer, watching the house. I called and told him a little bit about what was going on and asked him to call me let me know if he saw anything weird.

Sure enough, Charles called me and said, "There are several people out here, Sherry, and they have a locksmith ."

I called my stepfather and told him to get over there and see what he could do. Shaw had "called in the Militia" (who I'm sure was loving the drama) and Mr. Ed Haskell, that two- faced brown noser…One minute he was telling me every move Shaw made, and the next he was helping Shaw attempt to clean me out.

His love affair with Tomeika was shot to hell at that point.

The police were called. Legally, Shaw had the right to go in, but could only get his personal belongings. My stepfather made sure he only collected his clothes and then he secured the house. Shaw was served the next day.

A couple of weeks went by. Therapy was going well. I had to learn how to walk again like a small child and Mike was my teacher. We had a chant we would say as I took each step: "Advance left foot. Tighten the hip. Lock the knee. Right foot forward." (Then repeat.) We were working on walking with a four-prong spider cane and I tried to put everything I had into therapy. I realized Shaw's weakness was making me stronger...all I had to do was think about the pain and anger he inflicted on me and I could take another step. I made it work for me. Or I would think about my kids and I would take *two* more steps.

I was getting ready to be released from rehab, but I still didn't know what I was going to do. I debated hiring a caregiver to come to my house and help with the baby and myself. I also had to find a ramp for my wheelchair and get supplies for my home, like a bathtub chair and potty chair. It was overwhelming thinking about the things I needed just to function.

My mother and stepfather told me they wanted the kids and I to come to their house. They were getting some family together to build a ramp, and Mom was still on her leave and could help me adjust. They thought it would be financially easier for me to stay with them since I was still paying for my house, medical supplies, and lawyer fees.

I decided to take them up on their generosity. Boy, I don't think they had any idea what they were about to endure.

They, along with my father, came to the rehab hospital the day before I left to learn how to transfer me from one place to another, how to get me in and out of a car, etc.

Before I left, all of my therapists came to say goodbye. It was really hard leaving because I had put so much trust in these people. It was emotional. Mike hugged me and started crying. All the nurses came in and hugged me. Susan Berry came in and said goodbye, and that she couldn't stress enough how happy she was that I'd be going home with my mother and leaving Shaw. He would only delay my recovery.

My speech therapist also came to say goodbye. I said, "Tammy, I have a confession to make. I used word association to remember all those words you threw at me everyday."

She laughed and said, "If you had the problem solving skills to use that technique, there's absolutely nothing wrong with that!" She hugged me and said,

"You're one of the strong ones. You're gonna be okay. This isn't gonna get you!"

When my mother wheeled me out of the hospital, I took a deep breath of fresh air. I could feel the sun on my face and I felt thankful to be alive. I just started crying and could not believe how much I appreciated life. The things we take advantage of can be taken away in a split second.

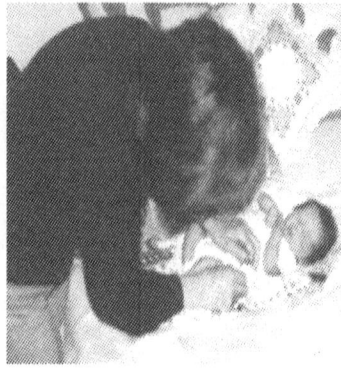

Mom, taking care of Gabriel.

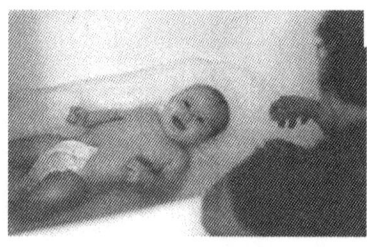

Mom, bathing Gabriel.

Mom, Codey and Gabriel.

*Codey, giving tired Mom
a hug after therapy.*

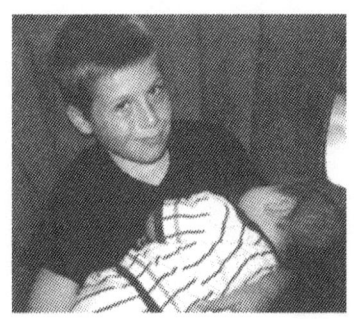

*Codey and his
"baby Gabe".*

Sherry L. Pierce

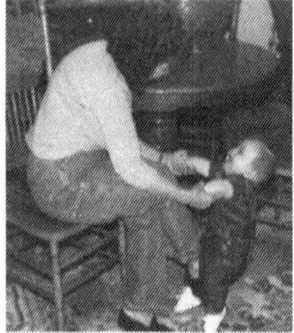

**Mom and
Gabriel.**

**My stepfather
David— who was
A huge support to
myself and the boys.**

Chapter 12

We arrived at my mother's house and I quickly realized that I had not been the one who bonded with Gabriel. My mother had.

She was there for him at all of those late- night feedings. I went through a stage of feeling a major sense of guilt for the pain I had inflicted on my poor family. I would look at my mother and see the pain and worry in her eyes. I would look at my father and see that he had trouble looking back at me. Not long after the guilt stage, I got really pissed. I'm not sure who or what I was so angry at, but if you got in my way you'd better hide, because I didn't care what I said or who the hell I said it to.

My mother's nerves were pretty much shot, between putting up with me trying to adjust to being handicapped and trying to take care of the baby and Codey. She was running me to follow-up visits with doctors and we were taking the baby back and forth to the pediatrician.

The baby had been throwing up a lot lately and having trouble keeping his formula down. The doctor ended up sending Gabriel to a children's hospital for upper and lower GI tests. The results came back and Gabriel was diagnosed with an acute case of acid reflux disease.

I had to rely on my mom to help me undress and transfer me from the wheelchair to the shower chair. She helped me wash my hair and bathed me. One night she was helping me, and I looked at her and asked her if she ever thought she would be bathing her 30-year-old daughter. She started crying and said, "I wish so bad this would have happened to me. It kills me to see you hurt and struggle like you are."

I look back now and remember that sometimes I would try to make light of the situation, and say something stupid to try to make my mom laugh. I had been having some headaches since the stroke, and was experiencing nausea and sometimes vomiting. It was scary because those were my symptoms leading up to the stroke. I went to see the neurologist: he gave me some pills for the nausea, but they gave me diarrhea.

I was going from the bed to the wheelchair to the toilet every hour on the hour. I bitched to my mother that "the doctor gives a damn cripple a pill to prevent the nausea that causes diarrhea and I have to do a wheelchair marathon to the bathroom every hour." She would laugh so hard she would have to cross her legs to keep from peeing her pants.

I began to realize I had to get myself better, and do things for myself. My mother was strong, but this could not have been easy on her marriage. Don't get me wrong, my stepfather was supportive, but this situation could take a toll on anybody. Many nights my stepfather would stay up with me and assist me with my exercises, and help me walk around the island in the kitchen. We had late night talks about how I was feeling and what we were all going through.

Shaw had hired legal council, and I received a rebuttal to my divorce filing. His lawyer, Mr. Will B. Debarred, was in my opinion an ambulance chaser with zero morals. He was ready to bleed Shaw and his ignorant family bone dry of any money they would throw his way.

Shaw denied that I was a fit parent to have custody of Gabriel, and stated that *he* was. He also wanted his belongings from the house. I was so amazed that this immoral family was even going to attempt to take my baby from me after everything that I had gone through to give birth to him. I stayed alive for my children and I'd be dammed if those bastards were gonna get my baby just because I had an unpreventable stroke due to delivering him. I was dealing with Satan and his helpers when it came to this bunch!

I was still very concerned about my son Codey. It seemed that everyone was overlooking him. The baby and I required so much attention, and he was left out of the loop. I started becoming angry with my mom. All I could see was her making Codey carry the bags. Go get this and go get that. It had to be terribly hard on "my buddy". I realize now that it was hard on my mother too. Before the stroke, I had spoiled Codey rotten. I laid out his clothes, fixed his hair, put toothpaste on his toothbrush in the mornings etc. This was a major shock to him because he did not have that anymore. I couldn't do it anymore, and my mom would not have done all of that for him. He was going through so many changes and I didn't know how to help him.

I started feeling as if my mother did not trust me with the baby. If she was holding him and needed to get a bottle or something, she would hand him to someone else or lay him down. She would never hand him to *me*. She would also take him with her upstairs at night, though I wanted to try to start keeping him with me. I was too scared to ask her because she was so attached to him, and I felt guilty trying to take him away from her. I felt like I owed her so much for what she had done for me and my kids, and I didn't want to upset her.

I had a follow-up appointment with Dr. Horn "Fart" and was interested in what he would have to say. I was very familiar with the Internet and doing research. (I had received my degree in computer programming just before I got pregnant, and I had my laptop computer). At night, I would do Internet research on strokes, stroke recovery, and my condition. I learned the terminology, and was able to come up with some questions about my condition that my family couldn't answer. I made a list for him and requested a follow up CAT scan before my appointment so that we could compare my condition then and now.

Dr. Horn spent a lot of time with me. He was impressed with how far I had come, and not at all surprised to find out that Shaw and I were splitting up. He told me that he was concerned from the beginning about how supportive Shaw would be and worried how that would affect my recovery. He said it was not very often that a wife lay in critical condition with her husband nowhere to be found.

He said he had never sat down and had such an intellectual conversation with a stroke patient. We talked about the damage the hemorrhage had caused to my brain. It mainly affected my left side mobility and my senses. I did not appear to have any left- sided neglect or cognitive damage. He said that my stroke was probably due to a condition called HEELP Syndrome, which is pregnancy related. My chances of having another stroke were close to none because I would not be having any more children. I asked him if he would write a letter on my behalf regarding custody of my son, and he said, "Absolutely."

I started goal setting and making a list of what I needed to accomplish to prove I was a fit mother (physically and mentally), and started working on them.

I needed to prove that I'm mentally capable

I called my rehab facility and asked the psychology department if there was a test to measure cognitive capabilities. They said yes, but it was expensive. It's not just for stroke patients, it's for anyone. It is like an IQ test, eight hours long. My health insurance company said they would pay for it if it was ordered by a doctor. The doctor ordered it for me.

I took the test. When I received the results, they said I was above average in virtually everything. I had no visual deficits or memory deficits. That was all I needed to check off the "mental capabilities" goal on my list.

I needed to prove that I'm physically capable

This one was going to take some time and effort. First, I needed to break away from my mother. No matter how hard it was going to be, in the end it would be for the best. I started spending as much time as I could with Gabriel. I made his bottles, changed his diaper, etc. I arranged for my father to come on the weekends, get the kids and I, and take us to his house so I could get some "alone time" with the baby. (I knew my father would give me the space I needed, but he would still be there in case of an emergency).

My mother was worried sick, but she really could not stop me. I was still their mother. Thankfully, Chris was supportive through these trials and tribulations. I kept him informed of everything I was doing, and why.

I bathed Gabriel, got up with him at night, and bonded with him. Codey was my best friend and my helper. If there was some kind of *"best son"* award out there, he should have received it a long time ago. I learned early on how important it was to not be bull-shitted, and I gave my son the same respect. I relied on honesty and broke it down for him, hoping his young mind could understand what I was doing. I explained that to keep Gabriel and to go home, *we* had to prove that *we* could handle this. He had a purpose. I needed him and he knew it! He and I became closer than ever and we became a team. Codey truly is my *anchor in life's ocean.*

I was going to an outpatient therapy program, which I was *not* happy with. It's somewhat hard to take a *300 lb.* physical therapist seriously. The first day I met her she was sitting at a table eating a box of muffins. She acknowledged that I had been wheeled into her room but finished her breakfast before saying, "Let's see what you can do?" Like I was a monkey that was going to perform a trick for her or something. I immediately had a bad feeling about that place.

That first morning had been a disaster from the start. Rehab had arranged for a handicap bus to pick me up in my wheelchair. I was experiencing firsthand what it was like to be out in the public as a disabled person. People go out of their way not to make eye contact with you. They walk further behind you to get away. So many people in this world need to stop what ever they are doing, take a deep breath, and thank sweet Jesus that they aren't disabled. Then they need to learn to have some patience and respect (not pity) for the people who are.

My biggest problem with my disability was distinguishing the difference between pity and compassion, and the difference between charity and a caring, helping hand.

I didn't want to be ignored or overlooked either. One time my mother and I had to go downtown to one of Gabriel's doctors. We had to cross a very busy one-way street. I was holding the baby and Mom was pushing my wheelchair. We had to go about two blocks. The whole time I was getting so angry, because nobody even bothered to make eye contact. We came to an incline and my mother couldn't push us up the hill. I had the baby, so I was unable to help with the lack of mobility in my free arm. She kept trying for what seemed like forever. I finally told her to take the baby, and gave it everything I had to make it up the hill. I was so angry because fullgrown men with nothing in their hands were walking by and not even giving us a look. I would have thrown myself out of the wheelchair and *dragged* myself up, just to show them that I did not need their help.

When we got to the revolving doors a very nice woman ran up to the door and said, "Can I help you get in there?"

In a very disgusted voice I said, "Would you, please. If my head were dangling off my neck by only a thread, nobody would even notice." I'm sorry for that, because *she did notice*. All of the other people didn't and I said nothing, but the one that did notice and went out of her way to help received the contempt the others should have.

Another issue I mustn't miss is handicap parking. It's there for a reason. So many times my mother and I couldn't find one. Once a lady pulled into one and ran into the store. I mean literally *ran* into the store. I felt like saying, Lady, if you are able to get out of your car and sprint into the damn store, you could park in a regular space." (So many times I had to bite my tongue to save my mother embarrassment).

When I was in this new therapy facility, I was very disgusted that they grouped all of the brain injury patients together. Mild, Moderate, and Severe. What better way to help someone with no cognitive damage get better than a:

Finger painting class?

That would have been fine if I was some sort of artist or painter, but I was more concerned about physical therapy and learning to walk at the time. My physical therapist was probably conducting some sort of home economics cooking class or something.

I NEEDED TO GET OUT OF THAT PLACE!

I needed to find a therapy facility that I could depend on to give me extensive therapy *and* involve the baby. I was working on physically proving that I could care for Gabriel.

My stepfather's cousin Chuck is a doctor, and we asked him if he could help. He was more than helpful. He and his staff were sent from GOD. We called my insurance company and made Chuck my "Primary Care Physician" as he suggested that would be easier for referral reasons. With my illness, I was seeing so many different doctors and needed a separate referral number for each visit. This is much less hassle if you know your doctor. He referred me to a new rehab. I'm not sure what Chuck told them, but these guys treated me like a queen. If I needed something, they got it. I was impressed that they had no intention of doing anything but physical therapy. No more finger painting and basket weaving.

I was sitting in my wheelchair when a very young, cute (but kind of shy) guy came up to me and introduced himself as Mike Barr. This could be good. My other therapist that I liked so well was also named Mike. I immediately hit it off with this guy. He was smart and knew his shit. I had by this time done a lot of research on stroke recovery and its rehabilitation aspects. I tested him every which way I could, and this guy was good!

My occupational therapist's name was Angelique Miller. She was also young and had such a sweet demeanor about her. We immediately started working with the baby. She was very impressed with my determination to get home and do everything myself. In the meantime, I had obtained letters from my neurosurgeon, neurologist, and had my cognitive test scores as proof of my mental capabilities and physical recovery.

We really worked hard the next couple of weeks at therapy. I decided I wanted to go back to my house for the first time and face the place where this entire travesty had started. I had a huge fear of going home for the first time, but I needed to start getting some of Shaw's things together for him to pick up.

They stressed in the hospital (when Shaw was still in the picture) that I needed to be made as comfortable as possible when I returned home, to ease me back into my familiar surroundings slowly. It can be overwhelming to try to go back to a life and a home with physical restraints.

To this day, I still do not know why he did this... when I returned to my house for the first time, everything was a mess. Pictures, flowers, lamps, and furniture were moved around or misplaced. It made no sense to me. My house was upside down. Shaw had a "Playboy" magazine on the coffee table. I had never allowed that smut in my house. *I mean, grow up Shaw! I have a nine- year- old here,* I thought.

Every drawer, cabinet, and closet had been rifled through. It was horrible; it would take me forever to make this my home again.

My dad came over and installed some railing on my back steps and in my bathroom. He also installed a vise on my kitchen counter to put my baby bottles in so I could tighten the lids. Over the next couple of weeks, my family helped me clean the house, rearrange the furniture, and make the place feel like a home again.

I had been worried about my father accepting my disability. He was so proud of me with my career and where I was in life. I felt like me having the stroke let him down. I do not think that now, but I know it still hurts him. My dad just wants what I want, for me to be happy.

One night, my mother and stepfather pulled out the couch (Shaw's favorite place to lay his fat ass) to vacuum, and we were grossed out to find a big pile of Shaw's nasty toenails. I could not believe it! He would lie on the couch, pick his toenails off, and throw them behind the couch because he could not muster up enough energy to take them to the garbage can. I have witnessed some nasty shit in my life, but I have to say that this one is a list topper!

I had the phone turned back on, along with the cable TV. On the phone bill, the week of the stroke, there were *eighteen* phone calls to Panama City, Florida. The bill was for over $200.00! I asked my Mom, "Who the hell lives in Florida?" We finally figured out that Shaw's hippy, drug- infested brother Caine was conveniently staying at my house when I was in the hospital. His tramp girlfriend was on vacation in Florida, and I was stuck with the bill for a brother-in-law I didn't even know!

I asked my therapists if they thought I was ready to go home. They were very supportive. My parents were a little worried, but I was determined. Codey was so happy. At my mother's house, the night before we were to go home, we sat up and just dreamed about being home again... with our own stuff, making popcorn and watching movies together like we used to. I was excited but scared.... I knew how crucial and important this was.

The next day, Codey was outside at my mother's house playing with a neighbor boy. They kicked a ball over the fence and Codey went to retrieve it. His shoe got caught on the fence somehow, and he landed on his wrist. He was pale as a ghost when he came in the house. My mother took him to the emergency room and we found he had broken his wrist.

Codey came in that night and said, "Mom, this don't mean we can't go home now, does it?"

I said, "No, buddy."

He said, "I could still help you with my other arm". I felt so sorry for him. Everybody had been telling him, "Now Codey, you help your mother". I told myself that I was not going to depend on my nine-year-old to be a caregiver. Maybe this happened for a reason.... maybe Codey needed some special attention for a change.

When we had his arm casted, I requested a waterproof one, so when I helped him bathe it would not matter if it got wet.

When I first got home, I was trying to figure out the best way to do things with one arm, trying to get a routine down. I was very lucky because Gabriel was a good baby. He did not give me any trouble at all. I would get up and work my ass off so I could get everything done before my mom got there. (At the beginning, she checked on us everyday). I could not sit down. Everything took twice as much time. I had to make Gabriel's bottles, bathe and dress him, clean the house, go to therapy and do the laundry. Over the next couple of weeks, I lost major amounts of weight, my endurance improved, and I got stronger. *This was the best therapy for me!*

I had my therapists come and see me at my home. They gladly wrote a letter concerning my physical capability in taking care of Gabriel and my home.

I also asked Chris to write a letter on my behalf, and he wrote the most compassionate letter I have ever read. I thought it would be important coming from the father of my oldest son: The letter read as follows:

To Whom It May Concern,

I have been asked to provide my opinion on behalf of Sherry Lynn Pierce. I have been involved with Sherry for several years, including our marriage from March 1990-November 1992. Throughout this period of time, regardless of our differences of opinion, personalities, and individual relationships, I would explicitly regard her as a competent, successful parent of our son, Codey Dylan Coke.

This decision was based solely on her ability to maintain shelter, provide consistent support for Codey's livelihood, and drive good values into his personality. In the age of divorced parents, such as Sherry and myself, it is easy for two adults to overlook the importance of family and their children. Sherry has always been there for Codey, as would be suspect for her infant son Gabriel. Her consistency provided, as well, in the care of Gabriel is a necessity for his proper nurturing and development, something that I am confident as a father, would be absent if Shaw were to obtain custody.

Sherry's assertiveness in developing herself academically, personally and moreover, dramatically recovering from a brain injury with nominal effects, provides precedence to extend her custody rights and allow her to proceed forward with her direct family.

(signed) Christopher D. Coke

WOW!!!

Yes, my ex-husband wrote that letter! I have three things to say about that:

1. My man picking skills had some potential!

2. Yes, This is my sweet Codey's father

3. If you are ever in a situation where it is in the best interest for you and for your child to get along with someone, do it!

I had the letter notarized and added it to my stack!

Chapter 13

I needed to obtain my own transportation!

I was getting sick of having to ask my mother and father to get me where I needed to go. My mom had already gone back to work, and I had to ask my dad to take me to therapy and watch the baby before he went to work. I knew that Shaw and his family would make an issue out of transportation in case of an emergency. I called my car insurance company and (in a roundabout way) asked my agent if a person with a brain injury would be legally covered. He said, "Sherry, your husband has already called me and told me about your condition. How are you feeling?" I thought, *Can you believe that asshole Shaw? He's not missing a trick.* All this time, I was keeping his car insurance paid (only because I didn't want to be liable if his drunk ass went and killed someone while driving), and he… for the wrong reasons, calls my agent to let him know about my condition!

Thankfully, it blew up in Shaw's face. My agent told me that it wouldn't be a bad idea to have a doctor's release, but he provided insurance to people with deficits everyday. Nothing was illegal about me driving. I went to my neurologist. He ran some perception and visual field tests and wrote me a letter releasing me to drive.

I still had the Prelude, which was a stick shift. I could not shift gears and drive with one hand. Therefore, I found an automatic Buick Century from someone at my mother's work with only 35,000 miles on it. It had power everything, and the keyless entry was very convenient. I took the last of my money and purchased the car. *I was mobile.* My therapist helped me find a way to get down the ramp safely with a stroller and the baby. This took a big load off my family.

I thought I now had enough evidence to back me up, to prove my capabilities for custody. I put together all of my letters and information and sent it to my lawyer. Shortly after that, Shaw's divorce strategy changed. We did not hear anything else about "sole custody" on his part. The new term was "joint custody."

Finally, going home…Too—Independence!!

Sherry, Codey and Gabriel returning to our home.

Gabriel, watching TV with big brother.

Mom, Codey and Gabe after we came home.

Sherry, Codey and Gabriel returning to our home.

Christmas (2001) Sherry, Gabe, brother Duane, sister-in-law Joy and nephew Billy. Also: Kelly, Danielle, Jeff, Carmen & Alysa

Gabriel

"Codey's Violin, sure plays beautiful music".

Papaw and Gabe after we returned home.

Chapter 14

It was still very important for me to set goals and meet them. I felt like I was continually being judged…an accident waiting to happen. I didn't want any help from anyone. My next big goal was to:

Become totally independent!

My mother was doing my shopping. My stepfather was mowing my grass. My step-grandmother, Ann, (bless her heart) was watching Gabriel when I went to therapy.

In a week's time, I hired a lawn service and started going to the store myself. (*That was an all day event.*) I was so fortunate to have "Granny Ann" watch Gabriel. She was the only person besides my parents that I would let watch him. She also helped take me to therapy before I purchased my car. I loved her watching the baby but she would not let me pay her. This independence issue was very important to me, so I talked to her about it. She totally understood. I interviewed, requested references, and hired a babysitter for Gabriel for the eight hours a week.

While I went to therapy. "Granny Ann" still watched Gabriel for me if I had a doctor's appointment or had to go to court.

I think my struggle for independence worried my mother. I tried making her understand how important this was to me. Looking back now, I can see her point of view. We were very dependent on her, and all of the sudden, I made her let us go. It was very hard for her.

I was wearing myself out. However, I felt like I was getting a little control back in my life. Shaw had been granted a motion to get "parenting time" with the baby on Mondays, Wednesdays, and Fridays from 6-8 pm and on Sundays from 12-6 pm.

This was a major joke. He only showed up when it was convenient for him. (Probably when "The Hand That Rocks the Cradle" Hagatha wanted to see the baby)! He continually filed motions for this and that. I know that he didn't have a pot to piss in, and Hagatha cleaned out piss pots for a living, but good ole Buck worked as a laborer for a Chevrolet plant and made decent money. I'm sure Hagatha was sucking him dry for the legal fees.

Two years ago, I actually thought Buck had balls. He started screwing around on Hagatha with a woman from his work. I wouldn't normally condone this type of behavior, but I actually felt like, *"Way to go Buck. I don't blame you at all, brother!"* It's hard to say what that crazy bitch did to make him stay, but he cowered back down and stayed with her. Hagatha has never been a person to keep her mouth shut. She had the entire family involved dragging him through the mud, trying to get pity from everyone. Hell, she called me at work one day and said she had a gun and was going to blow her brains out. I ended up calling Shaw and sending him to go calm her down. (Shit, I would give anything to be able to turn back time to that call)!

Buck and Haggy decided to "work things out". One day, Buck had an accident with a chainsaw and had to go to the hospital. His story was he fell out of a tree cutting limbs and the chainsaw cut his head. However, I have this mental picture of that gorilla Hagatha lurking in the damn tree, hanging down from the limb, grabbing the chainsaw, and gashing him in the head with it! "Throw Momma From the Train" performing

"The Texas Chainsaw Massacre." (She is three times bigger than he is and I bet she scared his ass into staying with a chainsaw)!

The lawyers made a date for us to arrange for Shaw to get his stuff. My stepfather and stepbrother Chris took everything out to the shed so Shaw would not be coming in the house. He entered our relationship with a Ford Tempo half full of shit, and left with two truck loads full. I was more than generous because I just wanted to get this over with.

My dad and I went shopping afterwards and replaced everything. I wanted my home and things as they were. I printed up a copy of everything he took, and my family made him sign it before he left. He was more concerned about his fish tank than anything. He wanted to know where his precious salt-water fish were. My father and I had purchased him the fish for his birthday! Well genius, lets see… you get some fish and no one feeds them or cleans the tank for three months. What would be the answer to that equation? *The fish are dead!!* We had a very nice Navy funeral for them: we flushed 'em!

Money for me was getting tight. I was on short-term disability through my employer, but was getting ready to be transferred to 60% pay. I was receiving zero from Shaw for the baby, and was paying for Gabriel's medical expenses and insurance premiums. I started looking into long-term disability versus medically retiring from work.

I filed for Social Security for the boys and myself, but this usually takes up to two years. Many people say it's very hard to get. You have to go through a lot of red tape to be awarded disability money. I decided that I would obtain a lawyer specializing in Social Security cases to handle the paperwork. .

When I went to see the Social Security lawyer, he said that my first application would automatically be turned down. This weeds out many of the freeloaders that really don't need to be on it. (I thought, *That's really fair. What about those people who truly need it but don't understand the system? Or they have some mental or cognitive damage?* They are turned down, and don't pursue it any further. I pray for those people). Unfortunately, our government is thus forced to stall on the truly disabled to weed out the bastards that are too lazy to work. GOD help us! He also said that with my very young age, I would be delayed in receiving benefits and probably be turned down a second time. *Like I asked to have a stroke at 30?* The more this guy rambled, the more disgusted I got. Then he said, we would go before a judge after a year or so, and have a trial.

He was to get a portion of my back pay, but I did not have to pay him anything up front. I indeed received my first denial letter, but on the bottom of the letter it was signed by my assigned caseworker. (She didn't have a clue what she was in store for.) I called her and introduced myself; I then told her that if there was anything I could do to help, to let me know. Every week I would call and follow up. If she was waiting on a doctor's report, I would call the doctor and get the information for her. She was honest and updated me every week.

I am thankful to say that my Primary Care Physician (cousin Chuck) was a saint, and swiftly filled out the paperwork they needed and provided them with the necessary medical information from the hospital.

My caseworker told me one week that she needed a series of tests done with their neurologist. I happened to have a follow-up with my neurologist at the end of the week: I asked her if we could use mine. She said, "I do not think that would be a problem, but these tests are lengthy. They have 15 to 20 questions, and they are very meticulous in how they are answered." I wrote down every question that she needed. For example: left arm range of motion, left grip strength, balance issues, etc. She said, "Do not be surprised if your doc does not have the time or cannot answer all of these questions."

I was in the process of trying to be weaned off my anti- seizure medication, and Dr. Frank was going to perform an EEG (This test measures your brain activity). Unfortunately, the results showed that I still had seizure activity and he wanted to keep me on the medication to be safe. He promised we would run another one in about six months, and see if we could discontinue the medication.

Dr. Frank had been my neurologist since the stroke. He teamed up with Dr. Horn "Fart" and was in charge of all my medications. (I really liked Dr. Frank: he was down to earth and very honest). I told him my Social Security situation. He shook his head, kind of laughed, and said, "You are something. Let's see what you have." I pulled out the long list, and he said, "Let's see if we can get these answered." It took at least 45 minutes, and we went through every question and every test. He said, " I'll get this report ready for you and let you know when it's finished."

It didn't really even matter to me at the time if Social Security accepted this or not... I knew this doctor did something he didn't normally do and went out of the way for me and that was really something!

I received his report and sent it to my caseworker. Seven days later, I called for my normal follow-up and found out that I had been awarded Social Security benefits, along with my kids. She was not available that day, but I spoke to her assistant, who said, "Wait a minute. This can't be right. When did you file?"

I said, "Three months ago."

"You have to be disabled at least six months before you can even collect. How did you get benefits so quick?"

I said, " Maybe I have someone watching out for me!"

She said, "I'll say!" Because I had received my benefits so soon, I was not eligible for any back pay. Therefore, I did not worry about contacting the Social Security lawyer I had hired. I had never received any correspondence that he had started on my case anyway.

I did get a call from him a couple weeks later to tell me that I had received my benefits. I told him I already knew and had found out weeks ago . He said, "This is an unheard- of situation. It's people like you that could put a lawyer like me out of business!! Ha! Ha!" *Oh, really,* I thought, *Milking the disabled is a respectable business to be proud of. I was, just fortunate enough to beat you at your game.*

Please don't get me wrong. I'm sure there are respectable people out there that help the disabled receive their benefits. I understand they have to make a living too. However, I just proved that you can receive your benefits in *three months,* versus a lengthy two years of zero money and $20,000 of your back pay. And I did it without paying this joker one red cent! You do the math!

Chapter 15

Shaw called me one night and told me he wanted to settle this divorce and get everything over with. He had only one question. "Why are we getting Divorced?" He asked, "People ask me all the time, and I don't know what to tell them."

I said, "Well, you could start by telling them you weren't there when I needed you the most, and then if that's not enough, you stole from me the first chance you got. I have a whole list if you have time!"

He said, "Well then, let's just get a F—king (He spelled it out)...DIVORSE!" Yes, it is spelled wrong, but that is exactly how he said it. I know, sometimes it's even hard for me to believe!

Anyway, he told me to make an offer and he would sign. I said, "Shaw, my main concern here is Gabriel, and I want sole custody. What do *you* want?"

He said, "Well, uh, I want the refrigerator, TV, a green Polo shirt, some knick-knacks from the house and stuff."

I said, "I will continue to carry Gabriel on my insurance, but I will be allowed to claim him on my taxes. I don't care about the material shit, Shaw. I want the baby to be a little older for overnight visitations. We need to work out a visitation schedule that we both can live with, and what is best for the baby." He agreed. I said, "I'm writing all of this down and you are telling me that you agree to this?"

He said, "Yes."

I said, "I'm going to have Brice (my lawyer) write this up."

The next day Shaw called and asked if I had called my lawyer. I had not yet. He said he wanted me to agree that he would not have to pay any back child support or medical expenses. We argued a little about that, not because of the money, but it really bothered me that Shaw skated through life when it came to everything. Someone was always cleaning up his messes or taking care of him. For once, he needed to at least be responsible for part of *his* baby. I in so many words told him that and he hung up on me. I was so pissed! I tried to call him back. He picked up the phone and took it off the hook. However, the line was still open.

I heard Hagatha in the background saying, "Shaw I told you, hon, that you couldn't make a deal with the devil! You need to stay away from her crazy ass!!"

I was in shock...First of all, I could not believe that I was actually overhearing a conversation that was definitely not meant for my ears. Secondly, she had the audacity to call me the devil? And finally, this moron cannot even manage to take the receiver off the hook right. Their conversation continued:

Shaw: "Mom, she's going to make me pay for the medical and back child support. I'm going to need $400.00 to pay her lawyer fees." (This was a lie: he was conning his mother) Cry! Cry! Sob! Sob!

Hagatha: "I know she's pulling some kind of scam on you, hon."

Shaw: "How?"

Hagatha: "I bet she's getting some kind of kickback from her insurance company!" (I thought, *Please, you dumb bitch! Get a little more original than that! You go to the doctor, they bill the insurance*

company, and the insurance company pays the doctor.
Where's my fuc-ing kickback? Good GOD! I cannot
cope with this insanity). "Shaw, you save your money.
I'll pay your credit card bills and give you the $400.00.
For all we know the baby isn't even yours."

Shaw: "Do you think, Mom?"

Hagatha: "Yes. Now let's go to the Hometown
Buffet for supper!"

That was enough!!! I hung up. The bitch makes a
statement like *that,* then her stomach growls and she
needs to go grazing at a BUFFET!!!!

I called Brice and asked him to write up the papers:
he did. He said Shaw and Mr. Debarred (his lawyer)
wanted to meet with us regarding the proposal. We
made a date and had the meeting.

At the meeting, we didn't get anywhere. Shaw
pretty much disputed everything we had agreed too. I
figure he listened to his family and then got some
advice from his ambulance- chasing lawyer and
decided to fight. Shaw rather liked the drama; in his
mind, this made him feel important. Sick, sick, sick!
He looked at my lawyer and said, I'm not signing

shit!" What a waste of time and money, and this was just the beginning.

Shaw called one day to cancel a visitation, complaining about having a sore throat (or some crazy excuse). This one incident sticks in my mind because he said he was thinking about having a DNA test done. I said, "That's fine. I think Jerry Springer does them for free. Maybe you can go on his show and take your redneck family too. They'll fit in just fine." Honestly, this hurt! I hurt for Gabriel; his father was trying to get out of paying, so he was not going to claim him. A light bulb went on in my head! *This is what I want,* I thought. *If he relinquishes his rights, I do not have to deal with these people influencing my son. He'll be better off without them.* I did not really care about the money; I always managed to make it on my own.

I called Shaw the next day and asked him if he would be willing to relinquish his parental rights. I honestly think he considered it, but Hagatha put a quick stop to that, I'm sure! They knew Gabriel was Shaw's. The hard thing for me to admit is that Gabriel looks just like his father. Nevertheless, that's okay he does not act like him and never will!

The fight continued…

Here is how our wonderful justice system works: The loser father gets "parenting time" to see the baby he abandoned, continues to work a full-time job but doesn't pay shit, and lives with his mother for free.

The crippled mother cannot go to work and only gets 60% of her normal pay. She furnishes and keeps up a household for the child. She pays for all the medical and legal expenses. And she gets to wait two months for a hearing at which the judge still allows the loser to go for joint custody. *Where is the justice in that?*

I finally received an order for child support when Gabriel was four months old. Shaw was to pay one half of the medical bills. I started receiving checks from his mother on Fridays. We had the maintenance hearing, and Shaw was ordered to pay $420.00 a month for disability maintenance, on top of the child support. This was unheard of. Maintenance would not usually be awarded after a six-month marriage. I feel that the judge's decision was swayed by Shaw lying on the stand.

Shaw was asked to submit his last two payroll stubs as proof of his income, which he declined to do. My lawyer called me before the hearing and said Shaw was not complying. I had to subpoena his paychecks from his employer's payroll department. (More expenses on my part). We went into court with the information we needed, without Shaw knowing we had it.

Shaw strolled into court, lied on the stand about his pay, and supplied the judge with a bogus check stub that showed he had only worked 20 hours that week. In addition, he had a letter stating that he was only allowed so many hours a week. That would have been acceptable if I had not known any different.

Shaw may have worked as a grease monkey oil changer, but he was the "Big Dog Grease- Monkey Oil Change Manager". Moreover, he somehow was allowed to make the schedules for himself and his felon punk friends.

Shit, I'm surprised those losers ever got anything done. But then again, how hard is it to motion a car into a garage and say, "Oil change in bay 1. Changing the oil in bay 1. Oil changed in bay 1. That will be $29.95. Car leaving bay 1." I still think it was a struggle for them!

His letter stating he was only allowed so many hours a week was, of course, written by one of his grease monkey buds. I guess you could say that all the oil changers of the world sure stick together. I do not think the judge really cared what letter he supplied and how loyal the oil-changing club was to each other. He took one look at our subpoena and made his decision. Credibility was definitely *not* part of Shaw's strategy!

Later, after the maintenance ruling, Shaw called me from a payphone and said, "You think you need disability maintenance now. You'll really need it when I come and break both of your fu—ing legs." It was somewhat ironic. After all this time and all the shit that has happened, I get the first glimpse of emotion out of him when I hit the bastard in his pocketbook. I bet ole

Hagatha was birthing a big cow about then! She *was* his main financial investor.

I filed a restraining order against him because he threatened me, but he denied it. Bless our justice system for this law; it seems the asshole needs to actually drive to my house and break my legs before anything would be done about it. I couldn't *prove* that he truly intended to do it . What a crock of shit!

We made over a dozen court appearances, and every time Shaw would stroll in right on time. One time, he was ten minutes late. My stepfather always took off work and went with me. We were always at least 45 minutes early. I sometimes felt like Shaw was just a charmed individual. It's like his irresponsible and idiot ways *worked* for him.

Gabriel had been sick with his acid reflux and I took him to the doctor. He did a routine check on him and found he could not get a normal count for his heart rate. He tried several times unsuccessfully. He sent us to a heart specialist, where Gabriel went through a series of tests: an EKG, drawing fluid from his spine, etc. (It was horrifying)! They ended up saying he had a "rapid heartbeat" and that they needed to put him on a home- based "Heart Holter" monitor.

I rented the monitor from the hospital and took the baby home. I was not allowed to move him at all because it would mess up the readings. I had to call Shaw to cancel his visitation and explain to him what was going on. Buck answered the phone.

In his defense, I have to say that Buck was very pleasant. He asked me how I was feeling. I said fine, and he said, "You know we all love you, Sherry". I truly think that this was Bucks way of saying, "I don't agree with everything that's going on" and I think he felt sorry for the situation I was in. Nonetheless, what he said seemed so outlandish I couldn't even stomach it. I told him to just have Shaw call me.

When he did, I told him about Gabriel's condition. He asked me if I had a doctor's note. This was so typical of him and Hagatha... not even the least bit concerned about the baby, just what kind of friction they could add to the situation.

My pediatrician was an angel. The ironic thing is, I found him through Hagatha. She knew I was looking for a pediatrician for Gabriel before he was born, and she worked at a nearby hospital as an aide. She asked around and heard about Dr. Lavra. He was in my area and "had a great reputation." Codey's pediatrician was twenty miles away and I wanted both kids to go to the same one, so I transferred Codey's records to Dr. Lavra. I have gone to him from the day Gabriel was born. He and his staff have been very kind through everything. They were aware of the stroke and that Shaw had left me.

When Gabriel needed his two-week check- up, I was still in the hospital so Shaw and his mother took him. That's how the pediatrician initially found out I had suffered the stroke. Shaw and Hagatha must have really put on a production because when I first took Gabriel to his office, one of the nurses said to my mother, "The father is really taking this hard, isn't he?"

My mother asked, "What would make you say that?" She told my mom that Shaw came in for the two-week check- up and was crying when he told them I had a stroke.

My mom told her, "Yeah, he's so upset he left her!" I think that after that, the office rather formed their own opinion of Shaw. When I asked Dr. Lavra to write me a doctor's note, he wrote a full-page letter. He stated both of Gabriel's conditions, that he could not be moved, and that Shaw didn't need to exercise his visitations, due to the babies health.

I wonder if Hagatha would recommend Dr. Lavra now?

In the next motion I received, Shaw was trying to hold me in contempt of court for withholding the baby from his visitation. He also wanted Gabriel's medical records.

I found out later that Shaw went into Dr. Lavra's office one day and demanded a copy of Gabriel's medical records. Dr. Lavra said, "No, the insurance is in Sherry's name, and she has custody of Gabriel. I won't release them." (Dr. Lavra is a spunky man that obviously doesn't take any shit). Shaw walked out, and in came "this big woman, kinda on the homely side, with ratty- like hair" "My son wants my grandson's medical records, and he has a right to them."

Hagatha's very highly recommended Dr. Lavra said, "I told him no! And I'm telling you no!" Of course, she would have liked him to recognize her, and even though she knew *of* him from the hospital, he didn't have a freaking clue who she was.

Shaw called one day and said that the judge would grant him the medical records because he and Hagatha were questioning Dr. Lavra's "doctorhood!" *Did he just say "Doctorhood"?* Click, dial tone. The ignorance flows out of his mouth so effortlessly and into my ear so violently. It's kind of like a virus that makes me instantly sick.

The interesting thing is, he was indeed awarded the right to see Gabriel's medical records... and the office said he never came to pick them up! Right there is a prime example of Shaw's disinterest in medical diagnoses.... he was just interested in the fighting and drama of it all.

Regarding, Shaw's contempt motion for visitation: the judge overruled it because I had the medical records and letter from the doctor to back up my cancellations.

The judge ordered us to go to a mediator to settle our differences. We went, and it was a complete waste of time and money. Shaw again wanted to owe zero money and asked for unreasonable visitation rights. He said his mother was a "nurse of pediatrics" in a nearby hospital and was more than qualified to help with the baby. Unbelievable! That uneducated bitch wouldn't make a pimple on a nurse's ass. She was as much of a nurse as Shaw was a computer engineer. He did truly go to school for that, but surprisingly didn't receive his diploma). "Ambitious" is not a word I would use to describe the career choices this family has made. I started praying that Shaw would find someone else to divert his attention away from me. Just go away....Crawl back under the rock where he came from!

Shaw was babbling about a TV, and asking me to change pediatricians for Gabriel. (I wonder why that was so important to him; could it be that Dr. Lavra had his number)? Unreasonable, he had no intention of settling.

After three hours of getting nothing done, I walked out tired, pissed, and with $300.00 less than when I walked in. We were stamped "mediation unsuccessful"! I even paid his portion in advance, because the mediator wouldn't see us unless arrangements were made for payment beforehand. Shaw was at another skating-through-life party!

Two days after the mediation, I received a motion Shaw filed to place me in contempt a second time. The interesting point here was he had filed this motion *the day before* mediation. My question is, if he had arranged to settle the next day. Why would he try to put me in contempt... to continue the battle?

Chapter 16

Shaw cancelled (or just didn't show) on his visits with Gabriel more than 1/3 of the time. After we made sure that the baby was ready and waiting, it was ridiculous that he had the power to put three people entirely out four days a week by not even showing up. I had made arrangements since the beginning of his "parenting time" for Shaw to pick the baby up at my mother's house. It was easier, I had witnesses, and I did not have to deal with his relentless ignorance.

He called from a pay phone on one occasion *forty minutes* after he did not show to pick the baby up. He stated that if I didn't get the baby back to my mother's (she had already brought the baby home) he would try to put me in contempt *again.*

He stated, "They won't know downtown who's doing the canceling and who isn't. It's my word against yours." (Translation for Moron: "downtown" probably means "The judge and the justice system").

I wasn't about to load the baby back in the car and take him to Shaw because his slug ass was forty minutes late. I told him to be on time if he wanted to see the baby, and left it at that!

When I received the second contempt motion, I asked my mother and stepfather to be witnesses at the hearing. I had always kept a consistent log of his pickups and cancellations since the beginning, and always had a third party there to make sure the baby was available. I was not at all concerned, because Shaw never had anyone with him when he picked up the baby, and he was too stupid and inconsistent to keep any kind of log. I did not think there was anyway he could get anyone to perjure themselves and say they witnessed an unsuccessful attempt at picking up Gabriel.

Think again, Sherry. "Raise your right hand" (A pause... I think it was an issue of not knowing her right from her left). "Do you swear to tell the truth, the whole truth, and nothing but the truth, so help you GOD?"

"I do," stated Militia. I will not use GOD to seek my revenge, but I wonder if Militia is aware of Judgement Day?

Militia has come to save the day! She would just do anything for her baby brother Shaw. I mean anything!

They had stooped to an all- time low (if that was possible). I knew what was ahead, and I was sick. I thought, *In this justice system, how do you fight pathological liars who have no life and truly love to fight? They stick together and scrounge up the money someway...yard sales, sell their livestock, banjo's and John Deere tractors to pay their ambulance-chasing lawyers to defend their crazy allegations.*

I remember a conversation I had with Margarita when I was pregnant with Gabriel. She was upset because Militia was trying to be controlling with Margarita's daughter, Sierra.

Militia doesn't have kids (and probably can't get anyone to impregnate her), but she wants to play "mommy" to other kids. I thought to myself then, *this would never affect me. I wouldn't let her get into a position to control anything that had to do with my kids.* Oh, how wrong I was.

Militia lied and said she had witnessed several times when Shaw was not allowed to pick Gabriel up. When asked for dates, they were unable to produce any evidence that they had kept any kind of log.

My stepfather was put on the stand with our log and stated that our log was accurate, and that Shaw never had anyone with him when he picked up the baby. Not only did we always make sure the baby was available for pick-up, Shaw did not show 1/3 of the time.

Shaw's lawyer put me on the stand and asked me if I had received any Social Security benefits as of yet. I asked, "What does that have to do with why we are here today?"

He stated, "It's a credibility issue."

I said, "Well, I've received my award letters but I have to be disabled for a certain period of time before I get compensation. So my answer is no." Then he asked if I would sign a release form so they could get the date from Social Security. At that time, I said yes, not realizing what this entailed.

Before the trial, I filed a motion that would place Shaw in contempt for not exercising the visitation rights that had been granted to him and for unpaid overdue amounts of maintenance and medical expenses he owed for Gabriel. The judge was going to hear all of these issues at this hearing.

This was unbelievable... Shaw supplied blank money order receipts for various amounts and claimed he indeed had paid me. He said he owed me nothing. He even made copies of cigarette coupons with handwritten notations like "11/12 paid $212.00".

We laughed at how ridiculous this was... First, a money order with no name on it does not prove anything. He was using these to pay his credit cards. Secondly, the amounts weren't anywhere close to the amount he was supposed to pay. Finally, his own handwriting on a *scrap* of paper stating he paid me a certain amount on a certain date meant absolutely nothing.

We laughed... until we got the decision from the judge. He did not hold either of us in contempt. He stated that I *had* proven that Shaw had not exercised his rights for visitation, but the court could not force Shaw to exercise them. All they could do is force me to make Gabriel available, which I had done (unless Gabriel had been sick) and proven. Here's the kicker... he ruled that Shaw had met his obligations and owed no arrearages in maintenance, but did owe back medical expenses. The judge had accepted his receipts. I could have appealed, but I was so tired of fighting. I needed to save what fight I had left in me for the custody battle. The money wasn't a huge factor. I can only assume that the judge saw the stack of crazy receipts and concluded that it would take an accountant seven years to figure the shit out. He decided to accept payment and deal with it later if I disputed receiving the payments. As I said, I decided I would put my money toward the fight for my son.

The judge decided Shaw and I would both have to have psychological profiles done regarding our parenting. He also wanted the profiler to see us interact with the baby. This was very expensive; it was going to cost $1500 for each of us. There would be two visits: an interview and series of tests at the first, and observation of our interactions with Gabriel at the second.

I made my appointment as soon as I got the order from the judge. It was a very long interview.

The psychologist wanted the whole story. I told him everything: how I caught him stealing red handed, why I filed for a divorce, etc. He told me that Shaw had not contacted him yet, and there was a great possibility he would not. (Shaw probably thought it was funny that I would be spending all of that money).

I knew if Shaw didn't contact the psychologist within a certain amount of time, his decision would be based on *my* account of events and submitted to the judge.

I felt that justice would prevail. If he didn't make the appointment, I'd get sole custody. And if he showed, I knew he wouldn't make it through the interview and tests. They were truly a challenge for just a *normal* person, impossible for an *imbecile*.

I arrived at the second interview with Gabriel. The psychologist chatted with me for a while. I told him I didn't want to bombard him with a lot of unnecessary paperwork, but I have always been the type of person that likes to back up what I say. I told him that if he was interested, I had letters from my doctors and therapists, printouts of bank activity when Shaw cleaned me out, proof that I have my own home, letters from my family and creditors that I maintained all of my bills throughout my illness, a letter from my ex-husband Chris, and copies of checks confirming that Shaw's mother pays his child support. He was very interested, and made copies of everything. He said, "You are very thorough."

He told me that he had received a phone call from a "John Mucus", asking what he charged for one of these profiles. He told him that it was $1500, and that it involved several hours over two visits, a lengthy interview, a 465-question test, and a take-home parenting test.

Not two hours later, "Shaw Mucus" called and asked that if his wife paid half, would that mean it would cost $750.00? (The court order stated that we were to each pay ½ of the total cost of the evaluations. The full price was $3,000. Shaw was just trying to figure out in his small pea brain if maybe the total was $1,500 instead of $3,000).

The funny part is that he only cared about the cost, so he did not want to reveal his real name in the first phone call. (But, he was too stupid to change his last name). He didn't understand his portion of the cost when the psychologist told him, so he called back and made an even *bigger* fool of himself by using his real name, hoping his portion would be $750.00 instead of $1500.

He told the psychologist that he couldn't afford that kind of money! The psychologist said, "Well, then I can't do your profile." (He told me that Shaw was not off to a very good start with his strange phone calls). Shaw asked, where his wife was in the testing. The psychologist said, "I'm not at liberty to tell you, but I *can* tell you she has paid her money."

The psychologist thanked me for coming in and said, "Sherry, I have to ask you to do something for me? If you're uncomfortable, I understand. Just tell me." I said okay. He asked me to show him how I would get Gabriel out of the stroller if I were at home.

I didn't even hesitate. I stood up, put my right arm underneath Gabe's back, leaned down, held him close to me, and picked him up. Gabriel laughed and started rubbing my face. It could not have been more perfect.

The psychologist said, "Amazing! How you manage with such a big baby."

I said, "The key is to keep him close to my body. If I go down, he goes down on top of me." (I learned that in therapy.) He told me he would get the report to the judge, and that it was a pleasure meeting me. I was so happy when I walked out of there. I was finally able to tell my whole story, to prove that I *was* capable of taking care of my baby. That made all of the difference in the world to me.

I have an opinion as to why Shaw never made his appointment. After I thought about it, it wasn't the money. Hagatha would have given it to him, just to continue the fighting. She had financed it so far, why stop now? The difference was that the doctor scared the shit out of Shaw when he told him the specifics of the profile testing. Shaw is afraid of his own ignorance. He was going to see a doctor that judge's personality and behavioral traits, and he has cheated his way through his whole life. Deep down, he was afraid what the outcome would be, so he bailed out.

If you put together Shaw, Hagatha, Buck, Caine, Militia, and Margarita's Intelligence, they still could not make it through tests like this.

Chapter 17

The psychologist wrote the judge a letter stating that I had finished my profile and that Shaw hadn't, and asked what the judge wanted to do. While we were waiting for his decision, I received another motion from Shaw. He wanted me to sign a release form for the Social Security office. When I looked it over, it allowed me to give Shaw permission to have all records regarding Codey, Gabriel, and I. I had a problem with signing over Codey's information. Shaw had absolutely no business having that.

I decided to call the Social Security office and ask them what information that they would be releasing if I signed the document. They told me that Shaw would get all of my medical records, work records, etc. I spoke with their legal department, and they advised me not to sign such a vaguely-worded document. They said that Shaw and his council were on a "fishing expedition", and that I shouldn't sign.

I told my lawyer that I didn't feel comfortable signing the Social Security release. He agreed, and said that unless the judge ordered me to do so, I shouldn't worry about it. The judge never signed the motion on the Social Security issue. He said he needed an explanation as to why they wanted the records. Shaw's lawyer said it was for "proof of income."

I had the Social Security office write me a simple letter to the judge, stating only how much the children and I would receive monthly. He accepted that as proof. I'm still not really sure why Shaw wanted all of our records, but whatever "Sherlock Shaw" had up his sleeve, it didn't pan out.

All we were waiting on at that point was for the judge to give us a trial date, so we could finally put an end to this divorce. In the meantime, one morning I had a knock on the door from two detectives and a police officer. They asked if Shaw was there. I said no. They said, "This is the last known address we have for him." I explained that he and I hadn't lived together in almost a year, and that we were going through a divorce. I told them that he would probably live in three different places over the next five years and this would still be his last known address. (See, here is how it works in Shaw's little bubble: "I will never take care of changing my address, so when I move, my creditors can't find me. That means I don't owe them anything").

They explained that Shaw was under investigation for a theft at his job, which he had quit. They had been looking for him all over, even out at Hagatha's (She had "no clue" where her boy was. "He did not live there anymore.") I told the police that I didn't know where he was, but that he picked up our son at my mother's house on Wednesdays. they could pick him up there. I was very happy to help the nice men with their investigation.

Surprise! That Wednesday, Shaw never showed up to get Gabriel. I did not hear from him for over three months. I started proceedings to charge Shaw with abandonment. Gabriel would be totally in my custody, and Shaw's rights would be revoked.

Meanwhile, I was really getting uncomfortable living in my house. It had so many bad memories, and I did not feel at peace there. I considered moving out of town, maybe back to southern Indiana where I grew up. I started looking at homes in Lanesville, Indiana, my hometown. I wanted my kids to go to the same small, independent school that I had. This town was overwhelmingly peaceful.

I found a beautiful, house that was perfect (from a disability point of view). It had a huge upstairs laundry room, and a garage where I could walk directly into the house with no steps. The master bathroom had a whirlpool tub with jets for my therapy, and a built-in seat in the shower. I couldn't have *built* a better home for our needs. In all, there was a two-car garage, three bedrooms upstairs, and three down. There was also a workshop, bathroom, and a living room in the basement.

I knew the house was too big for the kids and I but it was perfect. I took my dad on my second visit, and he loved it. We discussed it for days and decided we would try this venture together. My dad would sell his house and live in the basement. We would be there for each other. We closed on our house in Lanesville on March 29, 2002; exactly one year to the day of the stroke. The move of two households was a lot of hard work, but well worth it.

We only had been in the house for a couple of weeks when I received another motion. Shaw was putting me in contempt of court for not allowing him to see Gabriel, and for moving his child without consulting him. How ridiculous! He was the one who had stopped picking Gabriel up. The last I heard he was a fugitive, no one, (not even "Throw Momma From the Train") had a clue where he was! Yet, now he wanted to see Gabriel.

Right before we went to court for the motion, I had to allow my lawyer to give my new address and phone number to Shaw. Technically, he was still Gabriel's father. After my lawyer gave Shaw the information, not a day passed before I got a "poor me" phone call from the sniveling bastard. He said the theft investigation was over and that he was cleared of any wrongdoing. *I thought whatever! I can't believe anything you say.* He told me that he had messed things up so badly, and that he had been involved with another woman ("as a friend"). He had lived with her "as roommates" for the past six or seven months. He claimed they were just friends and convenient roommates. (She was only twenty, very immature, and extremely overweight). He just needed a place to stay because his controlling mother was driving him crazy. However, he could not live with this roommate anymore because she was "utterly filthy" and wanted their relationship to be more than he did. He said he loved me and missed us as a family, and wanted to get back together again. My feeling was: *If I have to choose between being alone (romantically) for the rest of my life, or settling for a romantically-challenged retard like this loser slug.... I choose being alone.*

We went to court on the motion. The damn judge resumed his visitations until the trial date. Because I had moved out of state during the course of a divorce proceeding, I had to take the baby *to him.*

When I wouldn't take his unemployed, broke ass back, his "friend" magically became his girlfriend. If Shaw ever told the truth in his life, it was when he said that she was overweight. She was indeed a very well-fed individual (and also a bit shafted in the looks department, if you ask me). I was graced with her presence when I dropped Gabriel off. She made sure that I saw her observing the child exchange. I think she was protecting her investment. Shaw can get very expensive for a workingwoman.

The judge set us a trial date. He thankfully granted me full custody of Gabriel based on the outcome of the psychological profile. The only unresolved matters that would be discussed at the trial were visitation, child support, and back child support he owed.

Sherry L. Pierce

***Our new house
in Lanesville,
Indiana.***

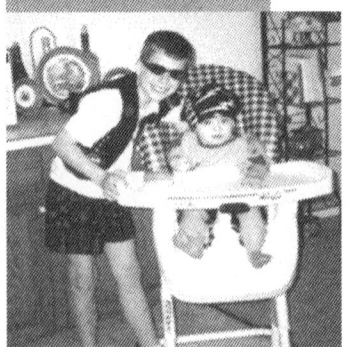

Gabriel

Too Cool!

Papaw and Gabriel at our new house.

Na Na at our new house.

Papaw and Gabriel

***Mommy—swinging
with Gabriel.***

"My wisdom"
and
"My Miracle"

Chapter 18

I decided I did not want to take the chance of the judge granting Shaw a visitation schedule that I could not live with. For Gabriel's sake, I offered Shaw a settlement. He owed me thousands in back child support and maintenance. He also owed me for half of Gabriel's medical expenses. I offered to continue carrying Gabriel on my medical insurance. Shaw wouldn't owe me any money other than $150.00 a month in child support.

In return, although I had been granted full custody, I wanted sole custody of Gabriel and full control over all decisions. In the simplest of terms, this meant that he would get to see his son, but couldn't say jack about anything else. With his past inconsistencies, I truly believed this was for the best. I continue Gabe's medical coverage only because Shaw cannot keep a job long enough to qualify for benefits. I think you have to be with an employer for a whole thirty days sometimes, totally out of the question for Shaw. Shaw was to take care of transportation, and I would claim the tax exemption.

What do you think he did? It's all about the Benjamin's!! I hate to admit that's why he agreed, but I speak for myself and my family when I say that it is for the best. It has been well worth it in the end. $22,000 in legal fees, the emotional agony of the custody battle, thinking these greedy ass cornballs may raise my son. It has all paid off.

On the trial date, my father went with me to court. We still had to present the settlement to the judge. We watched as a woman who had also suffered a stroke hesitantly sign her children over to their father. Regrettably, she was not as fortunate as I was in avoiding cognitive damage. I prayed for her. We were so thankful I was as fortunate as I was! The judge agreed to our settlement. It was over!

I knew, I would have never received a fair amount of consistent child support from Shaw. Although, my heart goes out to the shafted fat chick… she mails me a check for $150.00 of her hard- earned money every month. I thank her for that. When we receive it, my family makes a point of going out for a very expensive dinner **compliments of her.**

Shaw still cancels here and there. I wish, but do not feel, that he will be a consistent parent in Gabriel's life. I do know that the love and support that myself and family give him is enough. Codey has also become a true role model for his brother, and I appreciate that every day.

Financially, things are getting better for me. It was a ton of paperwork and doctor's records (almost as bad as Social Security), but I decided to take medical retirement from work. That was a very hard decision to make. In the prime of my career, I had to leave. However, I was in a position where I had to for the kids, and needed to for myself. Thankfully, I chose a pension plan prior to the stroke that would allow me a portion of my pay until I am age 65.

I found out later through someone at work that Shaw had checked on my life insurance policy when I was in the hospital. I feel like they were just waiting around at the hospital for me to die, so they could get what they could and take the baby. Why were they even there? Their actions proved that they really did not care about me.

Well, I'm still here, and I'm far from dead!!! Thank you Lord, for keeping me alive for my children and family. Thank you for giving me the strength to handle the pain and agony my husband and in-laws put upon me. Thank you for the strength to handle the effects of the stroke. Thank you for allowing me to keep my sanity through all of the insanity. Thank you for opening my eyes, for teaching me to take less for granted and appreciate what I have. Thank you for my boys and their unconditional love. Most of all, though I still have a way to go, thank you for allowing me to open the door and let you in for the first time in my life. I finally feel peace within myself.

Through the divorce, the custody case, and all the hell, I have continued my research on why I had this stroke. For legal reasons, I will be brief. I had some very important questions regarding whether or not it could have been prevented. After speaking with some specialists, it's still questionable.

During my research, I requested all of my medical records from the hospital and rehab facilities. I found out something that really scared the hell out of me. During my stay at rehab, Shaw had contacted the doctor on several occasions, stating that I was continuing to "talk out of my head", that I had "gone crazy", etc. The doctor questioned Shaw's motives, because he was also getting reports from the therapists and the psychologists about what was really going on between us. I truly believe that, with Hagatha's encouragement, Shaw was attempting to have me committed. What scares me is this: what if I would have had some cognitive damage? What would they have done to me? *It's way too scary to even think about!!*

I have had more good days and less bad lately. I'm much happier in my peaceful surroundings. With closure in the Shaw situation, my stress level is way down. I have more patience with my life and myself. I am getting better all the time. They say that most recovery from a stroke occurs within the first six months. I have to disagree with that. I see progression everyday with my continued therapy and determination. I believe that every case is different, and it depends on the individual and their circumstances.

I know I have a long life ahead of me. I'm going to focus on my children and recovery. In the near future, I have been thinking about doing some freelance work from home: building web pages or databases, programming, or writing a sequel (just kidding). It is important for me to apply my education and incorporate my schooling into my life somehow.

I am very pleased to say that when it comes to my mother, we have a more open, understanding, and loving relationship. We have more respect and warmth for each other. She was a little upset at first when we moved, but we are closer now than ever before. We see each other a couple times a week.

My dad and I are still just as close. He has changed in such a positive way; he is much more helpful with everything! He has a special closeness to the baby. He quit smoking because I do not like it around us. He even helps takes care of Thanksgiving dinner!

My brother Duane is a chief warrant officer in the United States Army, and was recently transferred to New York. We are closer than ever and talk all of the time. (I can tell by my phone bill).

Gabriel is almost two-years-old and is a healthy angel. He is one of the happiest babies I have ever seen. I must say that in my immediate family, Gabriel is kind of the "Golden Child". He is endowed with a special spirit I cannot explain. I guess it is because of everything we have been through surrounding his birth. I feel he deserves all the special treatment he can endure!

Codey is still my little helper. He just finished his sixth year of soccer, and started his first year of basketball and violin lessons. He is getting a chance to have some fun and be a kid again. I feel like he has had to grow up so much in the past year. He just started his first year at Lanesville Elementary (the school I attended), and of course made the Honor Roll on his first progress report. I am very excited to see what the future holds for him.

Codey recently won an award for a book report he wrote, called "One Bad Summer". It was based on his experience with the stroke and my recovery. We have *two* authors in the family. He asked me not long ago if we had any famous people in our family. I said, "Your great grandmother told me that the famous writer, Edgar Allen Poe, was a distant relative on my father's side."

He said, "No, Mom. We have you. You're famous."

I asked him, "Codey, How do you figure?"

He said. "You took care of me and baby Gabe *after a stroke.*" Right there, that let me know that I can quit trying to prove myself to everybody. I just need to be who I am, and that should be enough. I have the recognition I need, from the only two people I need it from.

My grandmother Marian asked me how I was doing the other day. I told her "I'M O.K., Granny."

Sherry L. Pierce

Codey 9 Years
Gabriel 3 Months

Codey 9 Years
Gabriel 10 Months

Codey 10 Years
Gabriel 17 Months

Gabriel Jacob

*Codey Dylan
and Gabriel Jacob*

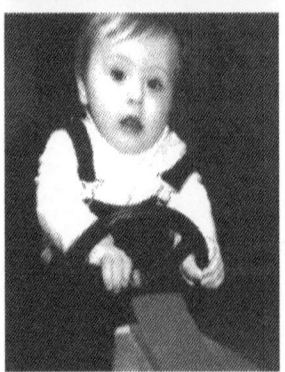

Codey and Gabriel playing on Na Na's International tractor.

Gabriel's first trip to the Zoo with his—Buba Codey.

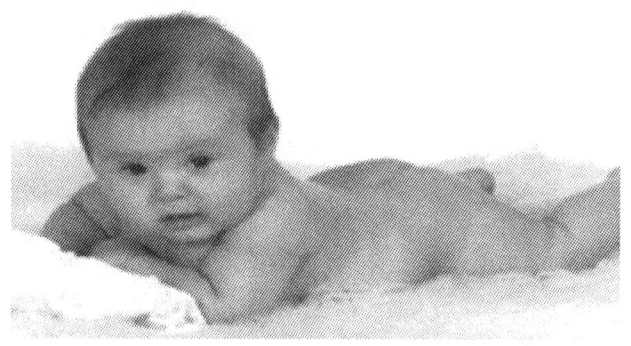

**I'm sorry, Angel—Mommy
Couldn't resist!
(3 Months)**

Some afterthoughts . . .

I'm absolutely sure that one day Gabriel (my true miracle from GOD) will have questions about his birth, my stroke, and what happened between his father and I. I'm a firm believer in not trashing a parent in front of the child. Unfortunately, the child will form their own opinions soon enough. When he is *much* older, I will give him this book. Although, his father and family will deny everything, you have to admit I would have to have one hell of an imagination to make this story up!

I release my anger for my health, spirit, and children. I believe that *everyone* will be judged. We are all here for a reason. In some form or another, every event that happens to a person on this earth is a test. How we react, and the choices we make, are all judged. No one is perfect, but GOD knows the difference. It all comes out in the wash! Or as Grandma Marian would say, "What goes around, comes around".

An interesting note: My neurologist once told me that the statistics on failed marriages of stroke survivors are astronomical. About 85% of the men are unsupportive of their wives, resulting in divorce. The interesting thing is, the exact opposite occurs if the man has suffered the stroke: the woman stays!

I cannot even begin to assess my situation in this statistical theory, because my neurologist said that my husband would have to had at least made *an attempt* to deal with my problems. Shaw did not live a single day with my stroke and its effects.

Please don't assume I'm bashing men here. Two men saved my life (my doctors). Two men taught me how to walk (my therapists). And my sons are going to grow up into two of the most decent men I'll ever know, because I will accept nothing less.

In my stroke research, recovery, and rehabilitation, I have had the opportunity to meet and talk with many different people who have suffered brain injuries or some type of paralysis. I have been asked for words of encouragement, hope, and inspiration. I would like to share a quote by a very well- known, intelligent woman:

"Franklin's illness gave him strength and courage he had not had before. He had to think out the fundamentals of living and learn the greatest of all lessons - infinite patience and never-ending persistence."
-Eleanor Roosevelt

"The only thing we have to fear is fear itself."
-Franklin D. Roosevelt

I added these quotes because President Roosevelt was confined to a wheelchair during his presidency after contracting polio in his thirties. He was, and still is, an inspiration to the disabled with his strength, courage, and success.

Now, for some advice from me:

"Use it or lose it" (anyone involved in therapy has heard this).

Continue your therapy as long as you possibly can.

Don't give up! During so many weak moments, I've just wanted to lie down and not get up, but I just keep thinking about my kids, my family, and how short life truly is. If you find self- acceptance, you will have serenity.

If you have any negative influences in your life, whether it be a caregiver, spouse, friend, etc....run! Get as far away from them as you possibly can. You will have enough negative feelings to deal with. It will prolong your recovery if you have to deal with someone else's bullshit!

Advise to any caregivers out there:
- Become educated about your loved one's illness. Know what to expect and you will be able to deal with it better.
- Don't take emotional outbursts personally. Step outside the box, though I know it's hard.

- Get some rest and relaxation (as much as you can).

- If you see any spark of your loved one longing for independence, be supportive. Allow them and help them to be independent.

- Don't talk around them, talk **to** them. (You would be surprised at how much they truly know what is going on around them).

- Find a support group or talk to somebody in a similar situation.

- Give praise for recovery. Our victories may not seem like that much, because it's stuff you would normally do without thinking about it. But we are learning it all over again.

- It takes a unique kind of person to be a positive caregiver. If you can't be 100% supportive, it is in their best interest to find someone who can be. It's not giving up, it's being honest with your loved one and yourself.

"The circumstances of every disability are different. Make the best of yours or it will get the best of you." -Sherry L. Pierce

My stroke has caused my family, friends, and myself a lot of pain and heartache. The stroke and its effects have touched people in many different ways, whether it has made them more appreciative of the little things, or just made them stop and take a look around.

It has not been totally negative from my prospective either. Besides adding to my appreciation of life and my children, it has somewhat enhanced my awareness and perception of my surroundings. I think more clearly, and choose to slow things down and notice more of what is going on around me. I have also become more in tune with my inner weaknesses and try to work on turning them into inner strengths. I pay more attention to detail, take time to listen to people, and avoid much of life's mental agitations and distortions. For example, I try not to allow myself to be pulled into worrying about things I can't control. I welcome any clarity in my life I can get.

I have realized that the easiest way to self-destruct is to give into anxiety, stress, anger, or depression. Easier said than done, right? True, but I just named four feelings I have experienced through my trials and tribulations. I can tell you that by letting go of uncontrollable situations and experiences, by turning that negative energy into positive thinking and using it in situations you *can* control, you will not only find peace and fulfillment, you will become a stronger, healthier person.

I'm not telling you that "forgive and forget" bullshit. I'm saying that you can't control people's words or actions. All you can do is try to understand what you're dealing with in uncontrollable situations, and come to terms with it. Usually, you're dealing with plain old ignorance. Leave it at that. Do not dwell on ignorant people and their actions.

I guess you could call it a sixth sense. Actually, since the stroke took my taste buds, they were replaced with an enhanced radar that enables me to detect ignorance when it is coming my way. So I have:

1. Sight

2. Hearing

3. Smell

4. Touch

5. *Built in Ignorance Radar Detector*

Chapter 19

This   chapter is an addition for my stepfather, David Schell. These are little stories that happened to me after the stroke that I'd like to share with you. not able to fit into the book in advance, I'll tell you that I hold no grudges or ill feelings toward the people involved. I fully understand that when we are born, GOD does not give us a choice of how intelligent we want to be. If that were so, I guess we would all be Einstein.

The Big Lazy Hair Dresser...

After my stroke, my sister- in-law Tina cut my hair and pampered me with aromatherapy and a pedicure. She does not live nearby, so about a month later I decided I wanted a perm to keep my hair out of my eyes during therapy.

I went to a salon and got the perm. I liked my hair, but the perm really dried out my scalp. (I found out later that my seizure medications had some side effects on my skin and hair). I went back to the same salon a couple of weeks later and told the hairdresser that my scalp was itching. I asked her if she had a product I could purchase to moisturize my scalp.

She started digging in my hair for a couple of minutes, and then motioned another hairdresser to come over. They both continued to dig, dig, and dig. It seemed like they rooted through my hair for at least fifteen minutes. (Please keep in mind that the salon is full of customers. Not only was I humiliated, but I had no idea what in the hell they were doing). She then put on some rubber gloves. *What's next?* I thought to

myself. *Get a damn oxygen mask while you're at it!*
You're not freaking microbiologist's doing some sort
of experiment. I just want to know what's going on!

I said, "Enough is enough. What the hell is it? Do
I have the fuc—g plague or what?" You could have
heard a pin drop.

She said, "I'm not really sure, but we think you
may have *lice.*" I thought, *What in the hell is going on?*
I'm in some kind of a time warp...I have a stroke,
which usually happens to older people, and now I have
lice, which usually happens to kids. You have to
understand, I am a compulsive clean freak, so when
this woman told me I had bugs in my head, I could
almost feel my left side itching (and it was paralyzed).

She told me (in front of the whole shop) that I
needed to go to a drug store and get some special
shampoo to get rid of them. I was so embarrassed.

I went to the drugstore and bought not one, but *two*
bottles of the shit. I went to my mother's house. My
mom and stepfather were hilarious. They didn't
believe I had lice, so they got out a *magnifying glass*
and started rooting through my hair. I did *not* have lice.

My moral to this story is: Do not ever go to a certain beauty salon and complain of an itchy head due to the perm that they gave you, especially not fifteen minutes before closing. They want to go home, not deal with your ass, so the last thing they'll do is admit they had anything at all to do with your problem.

Sherry L. Pierce

Nosey at the Neurologists...

Back when I was still in my wheelchair, I had a follow-up appointment with my neurologist, Dr. Frank. It was windy and rainy as my mother and I were leaving the office. She was pushing me, and I was holding the baby. My mother's intention was to get the umbrella ready, hand me the baby's blanket, and get us to the car as soon as possible.

Instead of getting up and being halfway helpful, or maybe opening the door for us, a woman sitting nearby said, "I would get a blanket over that baby's head if I were you!" in a rough, loud, snarly, irritating voice. (Yes, I looked, but no, it wasn't Hagatha).

My mother is not the type to make a scene. Moreover, as you have probably guessed, I have absolutely no problem doing that. But before I could retaliate, my mother said, "I have the blanket right here, NOSEY! Now, my words would have probably been somewhat more colorful! But I was very impressed with my mother's sassiness!

The moral to this story is: Unless your opinion is invited, keep it to yourself. If you are truly concerned about the well-being of another, first get your facts straight, then act. Actions speak louder than words.

Sherry L. Pierce

My Cane Plays Beautiful Music…

When I came home, I was very concerned about keeping Codey involved in his activities, and allowing him to be a kid. He decided he wanted to play the violin in his school orchestra. I was supportive because I was raised with a musical background. I played the piano and the cornet when I was in school.

I took him to a music store to purchase a violin. The line was long and the place was swamped. While the store employee showed me the violin, I leaned my cane up against the counter in front of me.

The next thing I know, this big, weird, white-haired dude comes out of nowhere and picks up my cane. He started looking it up and down as if it was a flute and he was getting ready to play it or something. I have no idea what the expression on my face was like, but I looked at him and said, "Do you want to buy my cane?"

He said, with a laugh, "Uh, no. I'm trying to quit." I could not believe this guy was so stupid. It is like someone asking you to move out of your wheelchair, so they can sit down. Later, the idiot came up behind me again with his wife and said, "Honey, this woman tried to give me her cane!"

She started laughing and said, "You need one!" I thought *Where is the humor in this conversation?*

I guess my moral to this one is: Leave shit alone if it's not yours. If you want to check out canes go to a damn medical supply store and leave the handicapped people alone.

Sherry L. Pierce

POOR CHILD...

This incident happened one of the first times Codey, Gabriel, and I went shopping on our own. Codey pushed the cart and I pushed Gabriel in the stroller, using it as a walker. We were doing fine... shopping, minding our own business, and feeling a major sense of independence. A woman walked up and bent down over Gabriel. I thought she was just checking out how cute he was. She looked up at me and examined me from head to toe. Then she looked back down at Gabriel and said, "You poor child!" and walked off.

I thought, *Does he look pitiful?* Gabriel was a smiley, jolly baby. What a hurtful thing for that crabby woman to say!

Moral: Please, please, please... if you cannot say something good...don't say squat!

*You Sure Are Fuc*ed up, Girlfriend!*

Right after I moved from my wheelchair to using a cane, I took Codey to a sporting goods store to get his soccer gear. When we walked in, a guy came up to us and asked if we needed any help.

I said, "We're looking for the soccer shoes."

He said, "Right this way"… and started *sprinting* down through the store. He woke up, turned around, and saw that we were approximately fifty paces back.

He sighed (like we were putting him out) and turned around and walked back. He said, "You sure are fuc*ed up, girlfriend. What happened to you?"

I thought, *Okay, you freak. I have a nine- year- old here who's intelligence exceeds yours by years.* I could not believe he said what he said!

And saying it in front of Codey *really* added fuel to the fire.

I said, "Yeah, I am. Go away. We don't need your help."

Moral: If you own any type of business and deal with the public, please screen your employees. Make sure they at least have a vocabulary before you hire them. I will never ever shop there again!

and one of my all-time favorites!
Fa La La La La…..Lost Your Layaway…

It was September and, never having been a procrastinator, I decided to do a lot of my Christmas shopping online. For what I couldn't do online, I went to the nearby, um…. "Q-Mart". I put some things on layaway for the kids. It was a very tiring experience, but I was thankful it was finished.

I had not been able to buy myself anything for a long time, and I wanted a camcorder to tape the kids. Q-Mart had one I really liked that had been discontinued and was without a box. I talked the manager down to an unheard-of price.

When I put everything on layaway that evening, the 12-year-old, snot-nosed boy working behind the counter was very intrigued with the camera, and asked me how I was able to get it so cheap. I didn't think much of our conversation until later.

I made my payments for the next two months and in early December, I went to pick up my stuff. They informed me that a mistake had been made and everything I put on layaway was sent back into stock. Needless to say, I was speechless. I wasted two more hours in an unsuccessful attempt to get together the things I had laid away. I was not surprised to find out the camcorder was gone.

Moral to the story: *YOU DO THE MATH...* SPEECHLESS & TIRED!

This last story is a catastrophe, but I can look back on it now and have a little chuckle, though I promise you it wasn't funny to any of us at the time. This doesn't have anything to do with ignorant people or their big mouths; this is just something that happened when I came home to my mother's house. I'm mainly sharing it because it's a huge reminder that "I have come a long way, baby!" I'm gonna call this one...

Uh…. help! Will somebody please remove this tubular object from the Asstroids on my Moon?

I was heavily into my "I'm so independent and I don't need anything from anybody" phase. (Oh, you're thinking I never left it, aren't you? I'm still kind of there, but I have come to terms with the fact everybody needs a little hand sometimes). Anyway, I didn't want my mother to help me bathe, use the bathroom, or get dressed. I didn't care if it took me three hours to get my pants buttoned, I would use the whole three hours, even if I had to become a contortionist and button them with my teeth.

I had a severe case of hemorrhoids from Gabriel's delivery. After showering, I transferred myself from the shower chair to the toilet to apply some hemorrhoid cream. While attempting to lean over to the left and apply the cream, I just kept on going. My left side was dead weight at the time, and I had some major balance issues.

I found myself crouched over the bathtub, buck naked, with a tube of hemorrhoid cream sticking out of my ASS! I can't tell where my left arm is, I don't know if I've done any damage to myself, and I'm in a position that if I unbrace my right arm from the tub, it will make matters worse. About this time, my stepfather David heard the commotion and knocked on the door to see if everything was okay. I didn't want him to see me, so I said, "Yes, but please get Mom *quick.*"

I'm sure it scared the shit out of her to see the predicament I'd gotten myself into. And when she saw the sight of blood, she lost it. (My knee had hit the shower chair going down and had a little scratch on it). She started screaming for my stepfather.

I cannot imagine the horrifying sight he had to witness when he entered the bathroom: my ass up in the air with a tube hanging out of it, with my mother (who weighs about a buck thirty versus my post-partum buck sixty) freaking out trying to lift me up.

I'm sure he was thinking, *I didn't realize this was part of the deal!!* (Just kidding). My tactful stepfather, of course, didn't say anything—he just helped me up and was very protective of my feelings. To this day, we've never spoken of that night.

I want you to know, Dave, that I know it must have been a ridiculous sight, but you handled it great!!

Yes, maybe I have had a tube of hemorrhoid medicine where I didn't want it…but I swear, my cell phone has never been anywhere near there!!! Ha! Ha!

Sherry L. Pierce

***I'm proud to say….
This is—My life!***

Sherry, Codey and Gabriel

Therapy, Therapy and more Therapy!!!

Apology...

If I've offended anyone with my slang, I'm so *damn* sorry. It was great therapy for me, my way of "taking care of my own shit!" This has been a very explicit way for me to express myself. I released a lot of anger on these pages. As you've learned, I've been known in the past to be "violent and crazy" (I can kick a mean pitcher of water), and I'm a little on the devilish side. It should make you happy that I chose to release my anger in this relatively safe manner.

Acknowledgements:

This part was the hardest of all to do… and the most important. You read a lot of injustice in the preceding pages, but the following acknowledgements express hope and love.. Everyone here has touched my heart and gone out of their way to be here for me. I love you all!

I feel the need to thank so many people for their kindness and support. I have put a lot of thought into this, but it is quite an overwhelming task. If I have missed someone, I am truly sorry. Know that you are appreciated.

When my family told me about all the concerned people that showed up that first night in the ICU, they said there was not enough room for everyone. My stepfather told me that it was amazing. I want everyone to know that it deeply moved me to know how fortunate I am to have people like *you!*

FAMILY

My son, Codey Dylan: "My anchor"

My son, Gabriel Jacob: "My miracle"

My mother, Brinda Schell and my stepfather, David Schell: "My caregivers" Thanks for putting up with my everything! I can't begin to list what you two have done for me, and what you continue to do for us. Thank you a billion times!!!!! I Love You!

My father, Loyd Pierce: Thank you for being here for the kids and I and for giving up the cancer sticks. It has been a long crooked road but you purchasing my "dream house" with me has given me peace. Thank you most of all for spending so many nights with me in rehab after you got off work. I know it was hard for you, but you were there for me, Dad! I Love You!

My brother Duane and family: Joy, Joey, Stevie, and Billy: Wayney, you were my first memory after the stroke! I owe you $160 for the airfare. It meant everything to me when you said I was the strongest person you know. Thank you for all the long talks on the phone when I needed you. I love you all.

Chris, Michele, and Alex Coke: I can't thank you enough for your support and love.

Marilyn Napier and Chuck: (Michele's mother and brother) Thank you for your concern and love for my son.

Grandma Marian and Curty: "My wisdom" (Skanny) I love you both. Thanks for being here for me.

Ann Schell: "Granny Ann" Your support, kindness and help are never ending. I told you once you were very close to my heart; I can't express that enough!

Chris, Tina, and Garrett Schell: Thanks for your love and support. Chris, thank you for the help with packing my stuff, moving me back home, the NINE ways to protect ☺, the dinner, and the movies, Tina, thanks for the makeover, your friendship, compassion, and love.

Chuck and Robin Trommler and family: Chuck, you went out of your way to be here for me! I have no idea what I would have done without you and your office. Thank you. Robin, Thank you for the food at the hospital and for being the kind lady that you are!

Kathe, Mike, and Kelly: Thank you for your continued support and concern. Kathe, your creativity on the bottle openers, etc. was not only helpful, but very appreciated. Thanks for taking the time to put that board together for me!

Dennis, Bubby, and Marcia: Thanks for the visit at rehab and your ongoing love and support.

Tomeika Lee, Breanna and Seth: "My cuz" Thanks for being my informant and for your concern and love.

Larry (Alias "Curly") and Vicky Lee: Vicky, thanks for the help with the baby in rehab and for all of your visits. Larry, you always had the most worried eyes when you would come see me. See, I'm okay. (Love you both!)

Scott Lee and family: Thanks for visiting in hospital. Just knowing you were there was comforting.

Darrin Lee and family: Thanks for visiting in the hospital. Just knowing you were there was comforting.

Ida Norris and family: Thanks for your compassion, love and visits.

Billy Lee and Joedy Satterfield: Thanks for your love and support, Billy Lee thanks for coming to see me, and for our talks. GOD bless you!

Amy Knight and Nate: Thanks for the visit at rehab and the gift!

Vanbree family: Trish, thank you for your support everyday at rehab. You were there for me even though you had your own ill child to deal with. You are a thoughtful person and I love you dearly. Mike, thanks for supporting Trish so she could come help me so much. I know you were taking up the slack with the kids. Erika, Matthew and Joel: Thanks! God bless your whole family. I pray for you, Erika! I love you guys!

Kenny Sanders and Megan: When you came to the hospital with Duane after my stroke is my first memory! Thanks for being there for me! I love you!

Steve, Jewelene and Jack Pierce: Thanks for your concern, love and visits.

Judy and Tim Kinser and family: Thanks for your love and support.

Jane Stockdale, Janette and family: Thanks for your love and support.

Mary Seewer and family: Thanks for your love and support.

Billie Jean, Leon and family: Thanks for your love and support.

Edward and Linda Sanders: Thanks for your visits, calls, love, and concern.

Aline and Lloyd Trommler: Thanks for your prayers, concern and love.

Sharon Trommler: Thanks for your visit, concern and prayers.

Helene, Steve, Matt and Bria McCormick: Thanks for your concern and prayers.

FRIENDS, NEIGHBORS, AND COWORKERS

Chester & Pat McCool: Your support and friendship went a long way. Thank you for your concern and help.

Lynne Farrisee: You were there for me always, bringing my check every week, just being the supportive person you are. Thank you!

Robert C, Susan P, Vicki G, Angela D, Aaron K, B.J. S, Stephanie R, Robert E, Barbara H: Your concern and visits are appreciated.

Gary Spatol and family: Your visits, calls, and concern were special to me.

Chuck Childress: Your persistence and help are appreciated.

Cecil: Thanks for your concern.

Jennifer, Rick, and family: Thank you for coming so far to see me. You're the oldest friend I have.

Carol Ghazi and Preston Cosby: Thank you for your friendship, love, visits, books, and phone calls.

Jane and Charlie Wade and Dawn: Thanks for your love, support, visits and talks.

Debbie Barnett: (Yale Kentuckiana) Thanks for notarizing my letters and for the visit and gifts.

Steve Keiser and family: Thanks for your continuing concern.

Mandy and Bud: Thanks for your thoughtfulness

Dorene and Sherdan Beasley: Thanks for your prayers and cards.

Elizabeth Long: Thanks for your many cards and prayers.

MEDICAL STAFF

Frazier Rehab: Your inpatient care was as pleasant as you could have possibly made it for me. Thanks!

Healthsouth Rehab: You are an unbelievable group of people. You are not only my therapists, you are truly my friends. I never want to leave ya! I'll be ninety years old, shuffling in to get my therapy from a stroke I suffered sixty years ago, because I have become so attached to you! Thank You!

Dr. Chuck's staff (Pam and Teresa): You made my referrals and appointments easy and you were and still are very nice to me. Thanks!

Dr. Dale Horne: Thank you for not having to do brain surgery on me after all. Sorry for calling you Doctor "Fart". Thanks most of all for saving my life. I want you to know that my family speaks of you with the highest respect for the way you handled explaining my condition and progress with them. I know that's your job, but I feel it was very important at such a confusing, emotionally critical time for my family.

Dr. Jeffrey Frank: Thank you for helping me with everything, and for your continued honesty.

Michael Barr (PT): I love our talks. You are a truly unique person and therapist. Thank you for treating me like your friend, not just a patient.

Angelic Miller (OT): You have been so good to me. Thank you for your support, therapy, and friendship.

Ron (PT): Thanks for your silly ways.

Jeff (patient): Thanks for the entertainment.

Eric Deyoung (OT Director): You have been very good to me. Thank you for your knowledge and understanding.

Diane: Thanks for making me laugh so hard I almost piss my pants.

Darlene: Thanks for your sweet greetings when I come into rehab.

Mike Shircliff (PT): You taught me to walk! Doesn't that feel good? Thank you for your knowledge, lack of bullshit, and support.

Tammy Pierce (ST): I appreciate your words of encouragement. Thanks for your therapy.

Amanda and Pam (OT): Thanks for your wonderful therapy.

Susan Berry: Thanks for the honesty

Angie Horrell (Frazier): Thanks for being my friend and for watching out for me.

Nurse Lenaya: You are so sweet and good to me. Thank you.

Nurse Brent: You are one HOT NURSE! Thank you for your talks and just being so damn cute! ("Would you ever consider changing professions?" – *Meet the Parents*)

Nurse Tracy (ICU): Thanks for shaving my pits!

Gwen (Frazier): "You bad girl". Thank you for your humor, motivation, and meanness. thanks for putting up with my shit! Quit the Newport's!

Dawn (Frazier): Thank you for the showers and talks.

Nicki (Frazier): Thank you for blow-drying my hair.

Dr. Livera and staff: I can't begin to thank you for going out of your way for my son Gabriel and I. You went out on a limb for me, and after being put in an awkward position that most people would have run from, you continued to help me through a very difficult time.

Dr. Haake, DDS and staff: Thanks for fixing my broken tooth. (I was trying to tie my shoes)! More importantly, thank you and your staff for your concern.

Dr. Karen Bloom (Frazier): You told me early on I would walk. You were right! Thanks!

Dr. Koferd (Frazier): Thanks for listening to me and taking time out for me.

Dr. Kraft (Frazier): Thanks!

MISCELLANEOUS, OTHER

V.G. Reed and Sons: (My mother's employer) Thank you for your kindness.

Clarke American: (My father's employer) Thank you for your kindness.

Schell Electric: (My stepfather's employer) Thank you for your kindness in allowing him time off to take me to court a million times. (Okay Dave, I know you let *yourself* off, but you did it for me).

EDS: (My Employer) You are so supportive! Thank you for your support and love.

Bruce B: (My lawyer) You put up with me for a long time. Thank you. And thank GOD I do not need you anymore.

Klondike Elementary: Thanks for your support and understanding.

Diane Bishoff and Jeannie Masters: (Codey's school secretaries) Thanks for your support and understanding.

Julie Herman: Thanks for watching Gabriel when I go to therapy. You are a big piece of my "independence puzzle".

Richard: Thanks for selling me the car that fit my needs.

Yvonne S: (Social Security) Sorry that I bothered you so much. Thanks for your honesty!

Bethel St. Paul UC of Christ: Thank you for adding me to your prayer lists.

St. Pete United Church of Christ: Thank you for adding me to your prayer lists.

The lady at Olin Mills Photos: You took wonderful pictures of my two sons together for the first time *and* gave us a coupon for 50% off so I could buy the whole package.

Thanks!

Wayne's Lawn Service: Thanks for helping me regain my independence.

The kid with the retainer at Hollywood Video: Thank you for bringing my movies out to the car for me. That was an extraordinarily nice thing to do!

The lady who helped me and my mother at the revolving door downtown: Thank you for making eye contact and for helping.

Hal Meade: Special thanks to the man who taught me "word association", the learning tool that influenced my life!

Samantha Kerce: Salon 250 Thanks for styling my hair for the cover of this book.

Avalon Photography: Barbie Adams and Margie Curtis, you completely went out of your way to photograph the most wonderful pictures of the boys and I. Barbie, Your photography is very professional and meticulous. You captured my vision of the cover exactly. Thanks a million!

Sammie Justesen: My editor. Special Thank you for everything you did for me while editing my book. Your encouragement and professionalism got me here.

Dee Justesen: My book cover was very personal to me...you knew that. Therefore, you made it happen. You designed me a very overwhelming emotional book Cover. Thank you!

Michelle Justesen: Thanks for your work on designing my book cover!

1st books Publishing: Suzanne Flinn, you made my book "live" Thanks!

Special Thank you to: My brother: Duane Pierce

My Therapist: Tammy Pierce

My Neurologist: Dr. Jeffrey

Frank

My Editor: Sammie Justesen

For being the first four people to read my manuscript before publishing and writing the wonderful "blurbs" for my book.

"We're O.K."

♥ *Our #1 Mom* ♥

Your smile make's us happy
You fill our hearts with joy.

When we are bad or in trouble
We are still your little boy's.

When you are sick, I can't sleep at night
I miss you so much, the tears I try to fight.

You mean the world to me and Gabe
You're the best Mom GOD ever made.

Please get better so you can hug us
And keep us safe from harm.

There's no place we'd rather be
Than snuggled underneath your arm.

XOXOXO

By (Your Son) Codey Dylan Coke

About the Author

•••••••••••••••••••

Sherry Lynn Pierce is a retired computer programmer who lives with her two beautiful sons in Lanesville, Indiana.

Along with enjoying quality time with her boys, she creates professional resume packets for graduating college students and is building a database system for a local small business.

Currently—and most importantly, she is designing a web page to educate brain injury victims and their caregivers. Contact Sherry at:

www.imokauthor@earthlink.net or

www.imokauthor@msn.com.